Ms. Moffett's First Year

Ms. Moffett's First Year

Becoming a Teacher in America

Abby Goodnough

PublicAffairs

NEW YORK

No part of this book may be reproduced in any manner whatsoever without written permission except in the case of brief quotations embodied in critical articles and reviews. For information, address PublicAffairs, 250 West 57th Street, Suite 1321, New York, NY, 10107.

PublicAffairs books are available at special discounts for bulk purchases in the U.S. by corporations, institutions, and other organizations. For more information, please contact the Special Markets Department at the Perseus Books Group, 11 Cambridge Center, Cambridge, MA, 02142, call (617) 252-5298, or e-mail special.markets@perseusbooks.com.

BOOK DESIGN AND COMPOSITION BY JENNY DOSSIN. TYPE SET IN ADOBE CASLON.

Library of Congress Cataloging-in-Publication data
Goodnough, Abby.
Ms. Moffett's first year : becoming a teacher in America / Abby Goodnough.—1st ed.
p. cm.
Includes bibliographical references.
HC: ISBN-13 978-1-58648-259-6; ISBN 1-58648-259-9
1. Education, Urban—New York (State)—New York—Case studies. 2. First year teachers—New York (State)—New York—Case studies. 3. Elementary school teachers—New York (State)—New York—Case studies. 4. Moffett, Donna. I. Title.
LC5133.N4G66 2004
372'9747'1—dc22
2004050535
PBK: ISBN-13 978-1-58648-380-7; ISBN 1-58648-380-3

FOR CHARLES PETER GOODNOUGH,
WHO TAUGHT ME THE MOST

CONTENTS

PREFACE

I first met Donna Moffett in August 2000, as I was finishing my first year as an education reporter for the *New York Times*. A new program was recruiting "talented professionals" to teach in New York City's most troubled schools, no experience necessary, and my curiosity was piqued.

Donna was one of those brave recruits, and she was among several whom the Board of Education put in touch with me that summer as I prepared to write a series of stories about the experiment. The idea was to shadow one of these career-changers, and to convey what it was like to enter teaching with the best of intentions and the most meager preparation.

Donna seemed just the subject I had hoped for: thoughtful and articulate; warm, yet emotionally complex. At forty-five, she had been in the workforce for over two decades, and had the restlessness of someone who had long suspected there was a richer life waiting somewhere. Most important, Donna was willing to give me full access to her first year of teaching, sure to be one of the most trying periods of her life.

In other times, the press-averse Board of Education might

have denied a reporter's request to shadow a new teacher. But Harold Levy, the new schools chancellor and the first to come from the business world, was calling for "transparency." So from September 2000 to June 2001, I chronicled Donna's experience at Public School 92 in Brooklyn in a series of front-page articles for the *Times*. This book grew out of that project.

Though I do not appear in the book, I witnessed most of the events in it. I sat in the back of Donna's classroom a few days a month during the 2000–01 school year, and on several more days in 2002 and 2003. She and I also talked on the phone for hours and met periodically for long interviews, going over all that was happening in Room 218.

There are several scenes I did not witness, which I recreated from interviews with Donna and, in some cases, with other people who were there. In those instances where dialogue was recreated, it was based on the memory of at least one of the participants.

To afford them a measure of privacy, I have changed the names of Donna's young students and their parents. Everyone else in the book, including teachers and administrators at Public School 92, is introduced by their real names.

It is important to note that most of the impressions and opinions reflected in the book are mine, not Donna's. While she generously opened her classroom and her mind to me, it was not her intent to cast judgment on her new surroundings, but rather to let me observe the New York City Teaching Fellows experiment from one intimate vantage point. Her loyalty to her students and colleagues is boundless, as is the dedication of so many teachers and administrators I met at Public School 92.

Ms. Moffett's First Year

CHAPTER ONE

It was just before 7:00 a.m., not quite rush hour on a Tuesday in September 2000, when Donna Moffett squeezed onto a crowded subway train heading downtown in New York. At the World Trade Center, where she disembarked, Donna moved with ease among the lawyers, stock traders, and office workers streaming along the platform. This had been her stop for the last decade, when she was a legal secretary for Flemming, Zulack & Williamson, and she still looked the part in her trim navy dress and modest heels. Today, however, instead of ascending the station steps, entering the cool marble lobby of One Liberty Plaza, and taking the elevator thirty-five floors to the carpeted calm and wraparound views of her former offices, Donna crossed the platform and boarded the express train to Brooklyn.

It was her fourth day of work as a first-grade teacher.

Just seven weeks earlier, prompted by an ad in the *New York Times*, she had answered New York City's urgent recruiting call for "talented professionals" willing to make a two-year commitment to some of its worst schools. The schools chancellor wanted new blood for these battle-weary institutions, people who were not only driven by altruism but who would be shocked—outraged, even—by the risk-averse, apathetic culture that pervaded the nation's largest school system. And so the New York City Teaching Fellows program came into being, an experiment born of noble-mindedness and arrogance, enthusiasm and cynicism, intelligence and staggering naiveté. For Donna and a few hundred others, it was a chance to do good—to enrich their own lives and the lives of children in need. And so they leapt without looking, into a challenging and tumultuous new career that bore little resemblance to anything that had come before.

All across America at the start of the new millennium, problems that had long beset public education had reached epidemic levels and were roiling the nation as never before. Aging schools were housing far more students than they had been built for, often in decrepit conditions, with inadequate books and supplies. Unruly students overwhelmed teachers, while parents, overworked or indifferent, shunned schools' appeals for help.

Budgets were ever tighter, and teachers were spending their own money on crayons and Xeroxes, books and field trips. An increasingly popular school of thought, perpetuated by conservative critics of public education, held that schools had been grossly overfunded and squandered the money, since there were no true sanctions for those who failed to educate. Prominent politicians like Mayor Rudy Giuliani of New York and Governor George W. Bush of Texas, soon to be president, were proclaiming that more money was not the answer; instead, they said, public schools should be forced to compete with private and parochial schools for students and tax dollars, through voucher programs.

Because of the harrowing conditions in so many urban schools, the middle class had largely abandoned them, departing for the suburbs or for private schools decades earlier. It was true: Without this vocal stratum of society demanding better public schools for its children, New York and other cities faced far less pressure to improve them.

If competition was indeed foreign to public education, there was no better proof than the teachers' unions that largely dictated how schools operated. These bargaining units, which had amassed great powers since their birth in the 1960s, all but guaranteed life tenure for the teachers they represented, regardless of their track records. They also required that no teacher earn more than others with equal experience, precluding school districts from offering higher salaries to those with expertise in shortage areas like math and science, or those who agreed to work in failing schools.

Instead, union contracts generally guaranteed experienced teachers the right to choose their own assignments, from which school they taught in to which grade or even which class they taught. Too often, this meant the neediest students ended up with the least-qualified teachers. Such mismatches were crippling urban schools from coast to coast, and this problem was just what New York and its schools chancellor, Harold Levy, hoped to fix—or begin fixing, anyway, for the road would be longer than Levy's tenure and that of his starry-eyed recruits in the Teaching Fellows program.

.   .   .

Some of Donna Moffett's initial fears about her new life had been about her physical safety. Would the commute to Flatbush—so symbolically far from her home in Chelsea—be dicey? Would she feel like an interloper as the only white person in her subway car, which she now often was by the end of her commute? Would P.S. 92, her new workplace, have dangerous stairwells and metal detectors at the front door? Now that school had begun, however, Donna's sense of worry and anticipation had shifted to the students themselves. As her train hurtled under the East River that morning, her mind filled with a very different set of questions. Would her first-graders be as happy to see her today as yesterday? Would they appreciate the stories she had chosen and follow the classroom rules she had posted? Would her heart pound a little less, and would it feel any less surreal when she greeted them in the schoolyard?

Around 7:40, Donna emerged from the subway into Flatbush, a sprawling, frenetic neighborhood at the center of Brooklyn. The morning was wiltingly hot and damp, and she was starting to perspire as she bustled down the two long blocks to school. Although P.S. 92 was less than ten miles from Donna's apartment in Manhattan, Flatbush—where Haitian-Creole, Spanish, and Arabic mingled with West Indian–accented English—felt so foreign that it might have been across the world. She had occasionally ventured to Brooklyn's few tourist destinations, to catch a performance at the Brooklyn Academy of Music or stroll through the botanical garden. But she had never had reason to visit workaday Brooklyn neighborhoods like Flatbush.

Once mostly Jewish, Flatbush had become a magnet for immigrants from the Caribbean, thousands of whom left beautiful but impoverished islands each year for a better life in "Bouklinlan," Haitian-Creole for Brooklyn. The blocks around P.S. 92 were lined with Jamaican roti restaurants and Trinidadian bakeries, Puerto Rican bodegas and Haitian hair salons. The side streets held low brick apartment buildings and wooden houses, packed tightly together, built in the early 1900s. To the west lay

Flatbush Avenue, Brooklyn's best-known thoroughfare, where buses constantly rumbled; politicians trolled for votes; and residents shopped, dined, and gathered on the sidewalks to gossip. Working class and bustling, the neighborhood lacked the menace and despair signified by the behemoth housing projects of Brooklyn's most desolate neighborhoods, like Bushwick and East New York.

On the corner of Parkside and Rodgers Avenues, Public School 92 loomed like a fortress, its pale brick girth surrounded by a green iron fence, its name carved over the heavy front doors in Gothic script. Opened in 1905, it resembled dozens of other New York City schools built around the turn of the century, their construction barely keeping pace with the great waves of immigrants churning through Ellis Island at the time. Sturdy and grandly proportioned, with detailed façades, huge windows, and ornamental flourishes, this building symbolized the value New York once placed on educating all its citizens. A century later, however, the school had a weary air, partly because of its lackluster surroundings. Across the street was a shabby Jehovah's Witness hall; next door, an apartment building of dark brick. Food wrappers cluttered the sidewalks; a sign on the school doors entreated, "Help Keep This Place Clean." A yard of weathered concrete, devoid of playground equipment and surrounded by a tall chain-link fence, stretched behind the school's graffiti-scarred brick. "No Barbecuing," another sign warned.

Donna was supposed to greet her small charges in this yard every morning at 8:00 sharp, then lead them through the intimidating building to their new classroom. She arrived just in time. The schoolyard was a sea of navy-and-yellow uniforms as hundreds of children made their way to the proper lines and fidgeted, jostled, and gabbed until the teachers led them inside.

The principal, Diana Rahmaan, stood sentry at one of the scarred metal doors, saying, "Don't push!" and "Hope you're on better behavior today!"

Donna was still sweating in her tailored outfit, obsessively counting her students to see how many had yet to arrive. How could she possibly keep track of twenty children she barely knew, among hundreds who were almost identically dressed? What was to stop a stranger from whisking one away while her head was turned? Just thinking about this possibility made her a little breathless.

.　　.　　.

One of Donna's first aims as a teacher was to learn the names of her twenty students as quickly as possible. To this end, on the first day of school she had reported to the concrete yard with her computer-generated class list in one fist, her camera in the other. The names on her roster were lyrical and exotic, bearing almost no relation to the Annes, Michaels, and Thomases with whom she had attended first grade forty years earlier at St. Raymond Elementary School in the Bronx. Shakeela, Jamal, Briella, Manette: Nearly all Donna's students were the children of Caribbean immigrants, and some had arrived in New York just before starting school. Donna was anxious to photograph not only the students but also their parents, in part because she wanted to recognize the person who came for each child at dismissal, but also to signal that she expected them to be present, in spirit anyway, as their children progressed through first grade.

Most of the adults who delivered students to her line in the schoolyard that morning had been polite but reticent as they met Donna, slightly taken aback by the new teacher's exuberant greeting. Still, all consented to having their pictures snapped, slinging arms around their children and smiling—some stiffly, some with amusement—as she clicked away. Some were not parents, Donna learned, but stepfathers, aunts, and sisters, even friends of the family. All but one were black; the exception was a white woman whose son, a sullen boy named Curtis, had olive skin and thick dark curls.

Donna had the pictures developed that first weekend after school began, and stuck them in an album with Winnie the Pooh on the cover. On Monday, she brought it to school, writing "FAMILY" in big letters across the front. Family was a theme of the first-grade curriculum at P.S. 92, and the album would fit in nicely with many of the lessons taking shape in her head. She stood the album on a corner of her desk and encouraged the students to page through it, saying, "We'll be writing about families a lot this year!" But it was also tempting to scrutinize the pictures for clues about the students' lives at home. Did Trevor's unkempt hair and pajama-top shirts mean that he came from a chaotic household? Was Jamilla, who towered over her classmates, truly only six?

Was that a nurse's uniform that Shakeela's mother was wearing, and did that mean she worked at nearby Kings County Hospital? Nicole's father shrank away from the camera, a pained, apologetic smile on his face, while Melissa's mom, very pregnant and with a huge grin, seemed almost to blot her frightened-looking daughter out of the shot. Little Curtis stared at the camera grimly, just as he often looked in class those first few days. Stefanie's mom, only half in the frame, seemed in a hurry.

A photograph of Donna in the schoolyard on this late-summer morning would have shown a petite woman, about five-foot-three, shouldering a tote bag stuffed with notebooks and teacher manuals. She looked a little younger than her forty-five years, with soft brown curls framing a round, pleasant face. Her warm eyes darted around the yard from behind small oval glasses with plain wire frames. She looked kind and motherly, although she had no children; only her smile, ever so tense at the corners, hinted that she was not entirely at ease.

Only eight of her twenty students had shown up by 8:00 a.m., but Donna still lined them up, shortest to tallest, for the march upstairs. Nicole Peat, a feather of a girl whose navy jumper seemed on the verge of swallowing her, went first. Jamilla Atkinson, the girl who looked much older than six, brought up the rear, glowering. The school was half a block long, dreary but clean, with windowless, echoing hallways painted light blue. Donna was learning to walk backwards, so that her nearsighted eyes could stay fixed on her brood. She stopped periodically to silence their chatter, bringing a finger to her lips and widening her eyes in emphatic slow motion. Most of the students were responsive, although Curtis rolled his brown eyes and heaved disgusted sighs whenever she stopped. Slowly the little group paraded past the brightly papered bulletin boards and banal inspirational posters that lined the halls: "Excellence Starts With You!" and "Our School's Building The Future One Student At A Time." Some of the building's grand original details could be glimpsed here and there, like the bathrooms' brass doorknobs, elaborately engraved with the words "Public School." The prevailing smell was of floor polish and slightly musty books—an oddly pleasant combination.

The horrors that plagued some New York school buildings, and that Donna had expected to encounter—crumbling walls, leaky roofs, burnt-out lights—were not present here. There was no metal detector, for those were only in place at the city's factory-sized high schools and a few troubled middle schools. P.S. 92, like most city elementary schools, had only a uniformed guard at a desk.

"Take off our jackets, take off our backpacks, take out our notebooks!" Donna delivered this directive in a bright, even tone as she snapped on the classroom lights and the students filed in. Following them was Ruth Baptiste, a young Haitian-American woman who had been assigned to Donna's classroom as an "educational assistant," or aide.

Room 218 was an ample square with high ceilings and three tall, paned windows looking out on Parkside Avenue. The floor was blue linoleum tile. The desks—actually small tables with four cubbies each—were new that fall, their decades-old predecessors, scarred with scratches and graffiti, now piled in a fenced-off area next to the yard. Barely a week after Donna had taken over the room, it was a riotous garden of color. Eager to make it her own, she had already added plenty of personal touches: A colleague from the law firm had made a curtain printed with bright rulers, jack-in-the boxes, and lions clutching notebooks, which Donna had hung over the door-less coat closet. She had also brought posters with lines from poems she admired, betraying her romantic view of the job that lay ahead. One was Edna St. Vincent Millay's "Recuerdo," describing an exuberant outing that perhaps symbolized for Donna the adventure she was undertaking:

We were very tired, we were very merry —
We had gone back and forth all night upon the ferry.

The other was Langston Hughes's "Harlem," which Donna had thought of often during her years at the law firm:

What happens to a dream deferred?

Does it dry up
like a raisin in the sun?

A plastic jug shaped like a teddy bear, filled with animal crackers, sat on Donna's heavy wooden desk in the back of the room. (She had been advised to relegate the desk there, since she would be on her feet most of the day and would have little use for it.) In the science corner, a miniature insect kit with plastic magnifying glasses and fake bugs adorned a round table, as did several toy badges inscribed "Park Ranger."

Some of the students took far longer than others putting their backpacks in the closet; Curtis disappeared inside it, peering out every few seconds with a clownish look, until another boy pointed him out. While some sharpened pencils and others whispered provocations to their seatmates, Donna stood at her chalkboard, writing her newly minted classroom rules for the students to copy and reciting them in the same bright, slightly tense tone.

"We will come to school by 8:00 a.m. every day," she said.

"I can't come by 8:00 a.m.," Curtis moaned, making a few classmates titter. Donna raised her eyebrows and looked searchingly at Ruth Baptiste, who only shrugged.

"We will enter and leave our school and classroom quietly," she said. "We will sit in our seats, listen carefully, and cooperate. We will raise our hands when we would like to speak. We will be polite, show respect, and use our inside voices. We will work hard and come to class prepared." During Donna's brief summer training, her instructors had harped on the importance of establishing rules off the bat. The rules, they said, should be as integral to a classroom as the desks and wall decorations.

She might as well have added: "We will not be scared." Because more than anything, Donna Moffett was frightened as she started her fourth day as a teacher, smiling resolutely at these children whose lives she was determined to help shape. She had tied her fate to theirs, or at least that was how important and scary this career change felt as she stood in front of these tiny strangers in the bright, humid classroom.

Donna's rule about arriving promptly had clearly not sunk in yet: Children continued to straggle in at 8:15, 8:20, 8:25. Some came with older siblings who pushed them through the door and took off; others came alone. As they copied the rules into black-and-white composition notebooks, Donna looked around and the tension briefly left her smile. "Since you are being so good—I'm so proud of you—I think we're going to have another party on Friday."

Room 218's first party had been on the second day of school, also a Friday. Apple juice and animal crackers and dancing for the last twenty minutes before the dismissal bell. A celebration, Donna had called it, for she had been so exhilarated and relieved to have made it through the first forty-eight hours. She would soon learn that P.S. 92, where nearly three-quarters of the students could not read at grade level, did not condone frequent parties.

A party? Stefanie Shaw jumped to her feet. Stefanie was the second-shortest girl in the class, with chipmunk cheeks and bunches of braids clipped with bright plastic barrettes. She was also the only girl who did not show up in the navy-and-yellow uniform that P.S. 92 urged but could not require students to wear as part of a citywide uniform policy that had begun a year earlier. School systems around the country had taken a page from Catholic school playbooks in the 1990s, adopting uniform policies on the theory that if students dressed neatly and identically, there would be fewer rivalries and distractions. Anecdotal evidence from some of the first districts to try uniforms, such as Chicago and Long Beach, California, suggested they improved attendance rates and decreased school violence.

In New York, uniforms were proving popular among Hispanic parents, many of whom had attended Catholic schools, and parents of Caribbean descent, who had grown up wearing uniforms to strict island schools. But since the school system had not outright required uniforms—that would incite civil-liberties challenges, system administrators feared—some parents, like Stefanie's, followed the policy haphazardly or not at all. On this day, Stefanie wore jeans and an acrylic sweater that would become her self-styled uniform, growing stained and frayed as the year went on.

Stefanie's eyes were like flashcubes, and they darted around the classroom constantly, never fixing on one thing for more than a few seconds. She charged to the front of the room and wrapped her arms around Donna's waist. Donna tried to shake herself loose, but Stefanie was steadfast. Donna took several steps backward; Stefanie still clung, dragging along. She opened her mouth wide to reveal a piece of bright purple gum. It was only 8:40.

.   .   .

No sooner had Donna succeeded in dragging Stefanie back to her seat that morning than Manette Petitjean, tall and thin with a lacy white kerchief covering her head, walked in, disrupting the class again. "All eyes on the board," Donna said cheerfully. Only a few eyes followed her directions. Under his breath, Curtis imitated her, scrunching his face and mouthing the words.

To start the morning literacy lesson, Donna again directed the class to copy phrases off the blackboard. One boy put his pencil down after writing a few letters and announced, "I can't see the board!" Another refused to get started, making Donna wonder if he even knew how to hold a pencil. A third boy quickly tired of the exercise and began wandering around the room, muttering, "Gotta go to the bathroom, gotta go now, now."

Stefanie, meanwhile, had snuck to the back corner and was trying to pry open the wooden cabinet where Donna had stowed the leftover juice and cookies from Friday's party. She was hungry, always hungry, and lunch was still a long way off. As the year progressed, she would clutch her stomach miserably, requesting chicken and rice in the middle of a math lesson or candy at dismissal. For now, though, a cookie from her new teacher's closet would do. Her hunger was making her bold and rebellious.

Suddenly, Donna's voice rang out from the front of the room: "Reprimands first!" she said, more as a reminder to herself than to the class, as she wrote Stefanie's name on the board. This tactic, gleaned from her few lessons in "classroom management," the Board of Education's euphemism for discipline, promptly failed. Stefanie cast a sly glance at Donna, then scurried to sit at Donna's desk. If she couldn't get a cookie, she would settle for her teacher's attention.

Trying a bit of humor, Donna announced that Stefanie was now the teacher. "Do you want to come up here and teach the lesson?" she asked brightly.

"No," Stefanie said as she rifled through attendance records.

Donna's next tactic was to ignore Stefanie, hoping she would return to her seat if no one was watching her exploits. But as soon as Donna continued discussing the months of the year, Stefanie appeared at the blackboard and grabbed a piece of chalk.

"Miss Shaw, do you want to write the word 'family'?" Donna asked, her voice growing higher and tighter. Stefanie shook her head and scribbled gibberish on the board.

In her old life, Donna might just now be catching the subway in Chelsea for the twenty-minute ride to work. She might have slept until 7:30 and lingered over the newspaper and a bowl of oatmeal, or even a plate of pancakes, before leaving her cozy, immaculate apartment. This morning, breakfast had been a piece of toast on the way out the door, and a cup of coffee from the corner bodega sat cold and barely touched on Donna's desk. But there hadn't been a spare second to miss it, never mind drink it. School had been in session for forty-five minutes; another ninety minutes to go until lunch, at the unthinkable hour of 10:15 because P.S. 92 had too many students for them all to eat at the normal time. Donna's feet were throbbing. The muscles in her throat felt wrung out, and her round face glimmered with sweat. She was aching for a moment to herself. She had one last, desperate idea: time for a bathroom break.

When the students assembled to go to the bathroom, they did not stay inside the yellow pieces of tape that Donna had attached to the floor at the front of the room—another tip from her whirlwind training, meant to mold packs of hyper students into an orderly line. Some students also chattered as they lined up, breaking a class rule. So Donna sent them back to their seats and waited, arms crossed, until they were silent. The trainers had warned her to be unyieldingly strict about the rules for the first few weeks, when the classroom tone gets set and after which it is hard, sometimes impossible, to change. They sat for what seemed like ten minutes, though it was more like two. When she gave the O.K., they jumped out of their seats so quickly that two chairs fell over.

"We're running out of time for stories," Donna warned.

The second attempt was more successful, and Ruth Baptiste escorted the students to the bathrooms down the hall. Donna was lucky to have her; full-time classroom aides were now almost unheard of in most city schools, thanks to budget cuts.

Urban schools everywhere had begun hiring aides in the 1960s as part of Lyndon Johnson's War on Poverty, typically choosing parents and other neighborhood residents for the positions because they knew the local culture and they needed work. But the academic contributions of classroom aides varied widely in New York, where they were not formally trained, were often poorly educated (no bachelor's degree was required), and had few duties spelled out in their contract (aides, too, were protected by the teachers' union). They were poorly paid, earning just over $20,000 a year on average, and many considered the job a pit stop on the way to full-time teaching or another profession.

The community school district that P.S. 92 had been part of before it was assigned to the Chancellor's District of failing schools had a disproportionate number of aides; it was one of many that had doled out these jobs for years as a favor to neighborhood residents. Because there were so many and they had job protection, Sandra Kase, the Chancellor's District superintendent, decided to put some of the aides in kindergarten and first-grade classrooms like Donna's, even though she thought many, with their lack of education, were more a hindrance than a help.

A motivated, enthusiastic aide could be a godsend, especially in overcrowded classrooms or among children with chronic behavior problems. In the best situations, the presence of a second adult allowed every student more personal attention, and the aide would work with small groups while the teacher instructed the rest of the class.

It was odd to share her classroom with another adult, but Donna welcomed Baptiste. Without her, more of Donna's early attempts to keep order in the classroom would have been as fruitless as trying to herd cats.

In the startling quiet of the bathroom break, Donna hurried to the back of the room to arrange the reading corner for story time. But her hard-won minutes of composure were almost immediately disrupted when the students returned and started arguing over who got to sit in the small wooden chairs, versus on the floor. The squabbling was apparently audible in the hallway, for suddenly Brenda Robertson, the assistant principal in charge of first grade, burst into the classroom and raised her right hand—the gesture used at P.S. 92 to invoke silence. Robertson's voice was far stricter and more foreboding than Donna's, and when she shushed the students, they immediately obeyed.

A breeze cooled the muggy room as Donna started reading *Jamberry*, by Bruce Degen, a book she had brought from home. Donna loved the book's rhymes and whimsical illustrations, and she had read it to the class a few times already. Several students had memorized the first line: "One berry, two berry, pick me a blueberry!" This was just the kind of scene Donna had imagined when she heard about the Teaching Fellows program. The students looked so sweet and enthusiastic, gathered at her feet with their chins up. Baptiste was smiling from her perch behind the circle, and even Robertson seemed to relax as Donna read, easing her disciplinary glare before she left the rapt class.

When Donna read the book's last page, about the author's memories of picking berries in the woods behind his childhood home, the students looked dreamy, as if trying to imagine such a pastime in Flatbush. This half-hour, at least, had been a success.

From the beginning, Donna liked story time best, and her enthusiasm was contagious. For the time being, Donna's students were still reading together in Room 218, which she loved because it seemed a calming, bonding experience for them. Soon, however, the children would be evaluated and assigned to groups for "Success for All," the strict reading program that every classroom in the Chancellor's District was obliged to use. They would be scattered among different classrooms for reading instruction—perhaps a good thing in that students would be placed with others at their skill level, but difficult and distracting for small children who savor the familiarity of their own classroom.

.   .   .

The following day, when Donna announced it was time for a story, most of her first-graders leapt from their seats and hustled to the reading corner. Only Curtis appeared unenthusiastic, slouching at his desk after the others had plopped onto the floor.

Donna had chosen *A Rainbow of Friends* by P. K. Hallinan, a book that celebrated differences like physical disabilities and shyness. In these first weeks, she wanted to impress upon her students the importance of acting like family—sticking together and loving and looking out for one another.

"Repeat after me," Donna said, using her new pointer to tap on words she had written on the blackboard. "Bonding means becoming good friends. Harmony. Richness. Friendly agreement." Curtis, still at his desk with his back to the reading circle, was stomping on the floor.

"Curtis, up!" Donna called. "Join the class in the reading corner."

"I hate that," Curtis replied.

"I'm sorry you hate it, but you still need to do it," Donna said, her tone gentle. She felt a particular tenderness toward this strange, moody boy with a mop of curls to match her own and a perpetual scowl. He had misbehaved more than any of his classmates in these first few days, but his grouchy comments were often strikingly funny and sophisticated. In a manner both endearing and disturbing, Curtis seemed much older than his age.

Grudgingly, Curtis left his desk and sat down behind the group. As Donna read aloud, most of the students paid such keen attention that her heart fluttered. Here were Luis and Stefanie, two of the worst-behaved students, jumping up to point out the pictures of rainbows and identify the colors.

Then, suddenly: "Curtis, why are you kicking Christopher? One of the things we're doing is bonding and becoming very good friends."

"He ain't my friend," Curtis mumbled.

Then, when Donna pointed to the letter *R* and asked Stefanie what letter it was, the girl shouted, "*D!* No, *K!*" But it was when Briella, a chubby girl with a sweet baby face, began sucking her thumb that Donna lost patience.

"Is this pre-kindergarten?" she asked, raising her voice. "Now we're in first grade. We're going to try not to suck our fingers when we're in the first grade."

This was a mistake; all eyes immediately focused on Briella and several more thumbs, including Stefanie's, went into mouths. There were a few minutes of chatter and reprimands before Donna started reading the book again. After a passage ending with, "A friend may be challenged in movement or speech," she stopped to explain that some people cannot walk and are confined to wheelchairs. In the back, Curtis murmured, "Good."

After another passage that began, "Each friend is given a share of our hearts, so no one feels different, unloved, or apart," he covered his eyes and shook his head. "Don't say that, don't say that," he groaned. Baptiste, sitting next to Curtis, said "Mmmm," and sadly shook her head. "My God," Donna thought. But she was not about to give up on Curtis that morning.

"Curtis, can you tell us what some of your interests are?"

"Nothing, besides sleeping," he said.

"Shakeela? How about you?" she asked a girl who seemed especially sweet-tempered.

"Sharing," Shakeela answered promptly.

"Sharing, that's lovely!" Donna said. In the back, Curtis added, "Sharing is dumb."

When the children were back at their desks, Donna asked each student to shake her or his neighbor's hand, as if ending a church service. Most followed her direction; Curtis put his head on his desk before limply extending his hand for Stefanie, his eager neighbor, to grab. The display of goodwill excited some of the girls so much that they jumped from their seats to hug Donna. Instead of reprimanding, she laughed. "I think it's very exciting to have love. Isn't it exciting to have love and smiles?"

Curtis rolled his eyes. But when Donna turned her back to write directions on the board, he silently reached back across the table for Stefanie's hand.

.   .   .

Frequently, in those early days, such blessed stretches of relative calm could fast devolve into chaos. Donna would move too quickly through a morning story or activity, and have fifteen or twenty minutes to spare before lunch. Exhausted, she would direct the students to the "learning centers" that she had set up in corners of the room: one for reading; another, with her insect kit, for science. A third, with plastic blocks and coins, was for math. Most of the children were noisy and jumpy; their attention spans had run out. Donna wished that P.S. 92 offered some sort of gym program; even though she had been there less than a week, she had already noted that her students were desperate for physical exercise during the school day. Their only recess time was the ten to fifteen minutes after lunch when they were allowed to play in the crowded schoolyard. Since there was no playground equipment, the principal activity seemed to be chasing each other in circles on the asphalt.

On this morning, however, the single student who had chosen the reading corner, Shakeela Jones, had picked up *Jamberry* and was thoroughly engrossed. She was quietly reading the book out loud, pronouncing almost every word correctly and shutting the noisy classroom out. She stumbled over "berry," but "jamboree" rolled easily off her tongue. Though Donna could claim no credit for Shakeela's ability, she was one-twentieth of the way toward her goal of having every student read by June.

Soon, however, disorder ruled the rest of the classroom. Donna passed out animal crackers from the jug on her desk, but a few boys grabbed extras when her back was turned, and the floor was strewn with crumbs by the time they were ready to line up for lunch. Just as they had before the bathroom break, the girls talked in line; even after Donna had sent them back to their desks three times, some were still talking. By 10:20, five minutes into the lunch period, Stefanie was scribbling on the board again. Donna asked if she wanted to be the teacher instead of going to lunch, and Stefanie shrieked like some high-strung tropical bird. Donna tried another experiment: writing "scream" on the board. The girl started crawling around the floor: If she could not eat lunch after waiting all morning, she would have to distract herself from her hunger by any means possible.

At 10:25, Brenda Robertson appeared in the doorway, raised her eyebrows at Donna, and silently led Stefanie out. Later, she would inform Donna that it was against school rules to keep children from lunch, even if they were misbehaving. It was among the first of many reprimands Donna would receive that year.

"I think you're finding out that I'm a strict teacher," Donna said to the girls who remained, her heart pounding harder than ever.

·   ·   ·

In recruiting the fellows, the Board of Ed had promised four weeks of training in August, then free, evening graduate courses during their first two years of teaching. It would take that long for the fellows to get a master's degree in education, and with it, the permanent teaching certification that New York State required.

Donna could not have been more enthusiastic when she had reported for training on August 1, practically swinging as she walked from the last stop on the Number 2 subway train in Flatbush to Brooklyn College, a surprisingly picturesque, old-fashioned campus where she and her "cohort" of about 100 fellows would be studying for their degrees. The setup, designed in great haste by the Board of Ed, the City University of New York, and the teachers' union, the United Federation of Teachers, was this: Each cohort would be divided into groups of about fifteen, and those groups would take classes together at their assigned college campus from 9:00 a.m. to 4:00 p.m., five days a week.

Then, from 4:00 to 6:00, they would meet with their "fellow adviser," a veteran teacher who would give them practical tips about everything from setting up their classrooms to navigating the Board of Ed payroll system. Along the way, the fellows would study for and take the Liberal Arts and Sciences Test— the most basic certification exam, which they had to pass before September—and get assigned to a school during a one-day job fair just for them. These were long, grueling days, but while Donna felt exhausted by week's end, the giddy joy that she awoke with each morning more than made up for it.

For Donna, like most of the other fellows, the daily coursework was like an unpleasant-tasting cough syrup. The reading curriculum, a jam-packed compendium of education philosophers like John Dewey and Paulo Freire, was partly meant to give the fellows a whirlwind tour of the values and beliefs that had shaped public education in the United States. Hundreds of pages were assigned each night, including densely worded chapters on brain development and child psychology. Donna dutifully highlighted passage after passage and took copious notes, but she and others in her cohort rightly wondered how all this highly theoretical information would matter when they were standing at the front of a frenetic elementary-school classroom.

Far more satisfying were the late-afternoon hours spent with her adviser, a woman named Monica Brady whose enthusiasm almost matched her own and who would be advancing from teacher to assistant principal at a school in the Bronx the next month. The sessions were fun and a bit silly: Brady would have one fellow act as the teacher and others as students to prepare them for quotidian challenges that had nothing to do with Dewey and Freire. They would practice lining up to go to the bathroom, walking backwards to keep an eye on the class, and checking the stalls to make sure no student was lingering.

Monica advised them to have a basket of bathroom supplies—soap, paper towels, even toilet paper—in their classrooms at all times, since school bathrooms were so often lacking these essentials. She urged them to have little rewards like stickers on hand, especially in the first weeks of school, as incentives for students to follow the rules. She warned them about the pencil problem—how children would use the excuse of needing to sharpen their pencils to leave their seats and wander—and said they should allow sharpening only twice a day, always at the same time. Donna, who had never spent much time around children, never would have thought of such issues. She was fascinated and grateful.

Monica had the group write responses to statements she wrote on a blackboard—statements that would prove immensely relevant to Donna's first year. "I am here to save the students," was one; another was, "My position as a Caucasian female will/will not affect my teaching."

"Who is anyone to suggest others need saving?" Donna wrote about the first supposition, though the idealism coursing through her veins compelled her to add, "I cannot save students in the vast sense, but I hope I can be a small part of a collective effort to make a difference. Tiny changes add up; the personal is political. I have enough optimism to believe each person can, and should, make a difference in the life of others."

Donna had been thinking hard about the race issue throughout the training; it troubled her that nearly all the fellows in her group were white, while virtually all the students they would teach and many of their future colleagues in the schools were black and Hispanic. The most time she had spent with people of other races was decades ago in middle and high school in the Bronx, where poor black and Puerto Rican children from the projects mixed, often tensely, with middle-class Irish and Italian kids.

"I must be realistic about what it means to be invited into a community that is 99 percent black," she wrote. "I will be an 'outsider' wanting to become an 'insider.'

"Yet," she continued hopefully, "despite awareness of race and gender, I believe we are all obligated to work individually and collectively to transcend these characteristics, to shed so-called identities which separate us, and to focus on our common humanity."

While the writing exercises got Donna thinking about the philosophical challenges she'd face, and the advisory sessions about the logistical challenges, three mornings observing summer-school classes gave her the only real taste of the life she was about to plunge into. The Board of Ed had arranged for the fellows to visit schools near their college campuses, in neighborhoods where they were likely to be working. Donna's group went to P.S. 92, just a few subway stops from Brooklyn College. Its status as one of New York's only schools to be categorized as "failing" for over a decade lent it notoriety, and the visiting fellows had no idea what to expect.

Once inside, though, Donna had been pleasantly surprised by the school's brightly decorated hallways and the warm welcome. The students—only about ten per classroom, because it was summer school—greeted the visitors with smiles and hugs, which deeply touched her. Little did she know that summer school, with its tiny classes, hushed hallways, and half-day schedules, was a teasingly false impression of how city schools really sounded and looked.

On the last of those three mornings at P.S. 92, Donna lingered to say goodbye to some teachers before hurrying out the front door to catch up with the other fellows. She felt joyful as she stepped into the blinding sun, but as she walked down the concrete steps she tripped and fell, tumbling to the sidewalk. Donna's classmates were too far down the street to notice, and nobody emerged from the school to help her as she gingerly picked herself up and gathered the notebooks that had sprayed from her tote bag. In that instant of searing pain, she felt suddenly, surprisingly alone. As she hobbled down Parkside Avenue to the subway, she felt humbled yet stubbornly clung to her hopes.

Chapter Two

In April 2000, Harold Levy was grappling with a crisis that would define his tenure as schools chancellor. New York State had finally ordered New York City to break its longtime habit of hiring uncertified teachers to fill the vacancies that sprang up each September in its most abysmal schools.

Technically this practice should have ended in 1999, when the state outlawed it. But New York City had originally flouted the ban. Although the state's education colleges turned out twenty thousand graduates a year, only a small fraction chose to teach in New York City. Even the city's own premiere teaching schools —Teachers College at Columbia University and Bank Street College of Education, which draw aspiring teachers from around the world—placed a mere handful of graduates in troubled inner-city schools. Between the low salary—$31,910 for beginners—and the common perception that New York schools were straight out of *Blackboard Jungle*, only the pathologically idealistic had much incentive to teach there. And the teachers' union, which had so much muscle that it dictated much of how the school system ran, forbade involuntary transfers and, until very recently, bonus pay for teachers who agreed to go to the most challenging environments.

New York was not unique: Whether out of fear, prejudice, burnout, or indifference to the plight of poor minority children, the nation's largely white teaching force had never made a priority of failing schools in isolated neighborhoods. Race was a huge, if largely unspoken, issue: The students in failing schools were virtually all black and Hispanic, while more seasoned teachers were still overwhelmingly white and lived in white, middle-class neighborhoods. Many teachers were afraid to even set foot in the neighborhoods where the worst schools were found, imagining they would be mugged or their cars stripped in broad daylight. They also feared the students, who they assumed were menacing at worst, apathetic at best, and impossible to teach. The few who did take up the challenge tended to quickly change their minds: A quarter of the teachers in New York's failing schools left each year, compared with only eight percent in the city's other schools. Only a handful stayed longer than three years. To fill the gap, the Board of Ed had been forced to hire uncertified teachers.

The problem was by now endemic to urban school districts, for the days when teaching was the best and often only option for college-educated women were long gone. Once a guarantee of a healthy middle-class existence, teacher salaries had not kept pace with those in the private sector—the average starting salary for public school teachers in September 2000 was $26,845, compared with $37,255 in public accounting, $33,143 in sales, and $49,111 in chemical engineering. While scores of the nation's brightest women had pursued teaching careers in the 1950s, joined in the late '60s and early '70s by a cadre of highly educated men seeking to avoid Vietnam, the modern teaching candidate was typically not an academic star.

True, every generation had a corps of self-sacrificing do-gooders intent on making their mark through teaching. But they were the exception in a field that now attracted too many mediocre minds. Just how many new teachers were sub par was hard to quantify, though one study found that college graduates whose SAT or ACT scores were in the bottom quartile were more than twice as likely as those in the top quartile to have majored in education. For too many, the stability of teaching—the easy path in, the sturdy pensions and health benefits, the job security—was a bigger draw than its intellectual challenges.

In 2000, as in past boom years, headlines were blaring warnings of a national teaching shortage. Sure enough, the spectacular economy of the late '90s had made teaching an even less attractive option to new college graduates, and school districts from Seattle to Miami were predicting record vacancies as a result. Between growing enrollments, efforts to reduce class size, and the imminent retirement of hundreds of thousands of women who entered teaching in the '50s and '60s, the nation's public schools were expecting to need up to 2.2 million new teachers by 2012—almost as many as the 2.8 million now working.

For now, though, the problem was not so much a lack of candidates as of *strong* candidates, and the tendency of new teachers to leave within their first few years on the job. Bright, creative types were often the first to go, because they could not stand the constraining work rules—excessive paperwork, for example—that schools were now imposing to keep weak teachers in check. And too often, uncertified teachers were taking their place. Twenty-three percent of teachers in California's high-poverty school districts would lack basic certification in 2000–01, as would 23 percent in Louisiana's, 19 percent in Maryland's, 18 percent in North Carolina's, and 17 percent in New York's. For new teachers, the percentages would generally be much higher.

Though some uncertified teachers proved excellent at the job, as a group, they were woefully underqualified. In New York, many had repeatedly failed the Liberal Arts and Sciences Test, the most general of the three exams the state requires for certification. Others had not finished or even begun the requisite education courses, or completed even a day of student teaching. But all they needed for a temporary teaching license was a bachelor's degree in any subject and a criminal background check. To fill the several hundred openings in failing schools each fall, the joke went, principals used the fogged-mirror test: If a mirror held to the applicant's mouth fogged, the applicant was breathing and thereby equipped to teach in Harlem, Flatbush, or the South Bronx.

Not surprisingly, the roughly one hundred city schools categorized as failing had far more uncertified teachers than their better-performing counterparts: A whopping 80 percent of the teachers hired in failing schools during the 1990s lacked certification, and were working with emergency credentials. Rick Mills, the state education commissioner, believed they were the main reason for the schools' terrible performance. While their licenses were supposed to be temporary, these teachers often got to stay on the job indefinitely without earning permanent certification, because no one better came along to take their place.

Once they did get certified, it was for life. Though some politicians and think tanks had proposed periodic re-testing for all teachers, unions had rejected the idea, saying it would result in weak teachers losing their jobs instead of getting the extra coaching and support that was their due.

Harold Levy had served on the State Board of Regents, a group of political appointees who created education policy alongside the commissioner, before becoming chancellor. As a regent, Levy had enthusiastically—and naively, he realized in retrospect—voted for New York's ban on uncertified teachers. Where was he going to find a few hundred fully qualified teachers willing to work in schools that the tabloid newspapers called "Worst of the Worst" and "Halls of Shame"? He laid out the bleak situation in a letter to Mills that April, requesting a waiver from the ban for the coming fall. Mills remained adamant, however. Not only would he deny a waiver, he wrote Levy back, he might also sue the Board of Ed to enforce the ban.

Mills had a lot riding on the hiring policy, one of many headline-grabbing changes that he and the Board of Regents had made in a bold effort to raise the achievement bar for both students and teachers. New York was a leader in the national movement toward more rigorous academic requirements. Proud of the example he had set, Mills did not want to be caught retreating—though a case could be made that he had set the bar too high, too fast.

Levy was in an awkward position. He had pledged to make teacher recruitment the top priority of his tenure. Like Mills, he thought hiring smarter, more energetic teachers the biggest key to improving inner-city schools. Fighting Mills and his policy would make Levy look like a hypocrite—just another "educrat" defending the status quo. As the school system's first chancellor from the corporate world, hired on the premise that he would shake things up, Levy could not afford to be seen that way.

. . .

As soon as he received Mills's threatening letter on April 7, Levy began obsessing about how to meet his demand, picking his aides' brains for ideas. He had exactly five months to comply, an infinitesimal amount of time in a system so moribund it sometimes took years to fix even minor problems. Orders flowed rigidly from the top—the largest government bureaucracy outside Washington, according to education historian Diane Ravitch—dictating spending, hiring, and building-maintenance decisions with minimal flexibility. Between this mammoth central administration of roughly 3,200 employees and the thirty-two community school boards, the teachers' and principals' unions, and local politicians, who all demanded a say in education decisions, changing something like a teacher-hiring policy was like turning around a battleship. School bureaucracies elsewhere were equally resistant to change, but the sheer size of the New York system made innovation a particularly tall order.

One of Levy's aides was Vicki Bernstein, a quiet, intense woman who had worked as a policy analyst for the previous chancellor and was hungry for a new assignment. In early April, Bernstein told Levy of a plan that her old boss had mulled, but never acted on: recruiting people from other careers, giving them a crash course in teaching, then sending them to graduate school while they taught. It was not a new concept; other cities and states, including New Jersey, Connecticut, and Texas, had already created so-called "alternate routes" to teaching. Bernstein thought that such an unorthodox approach might attract New Yorkers who were interested in becoming teachers but put off by the idea of having to return to school first.

Bernstein's suggestion immediately appealed to Levy, who already believed that many education school graduates were not up to par intellectually. He had seen data indicating that teachers' SAT scores were not only generally lower than other professionals', but also were dropping from year to year. Levy believed that the Board of Ed should be wooing graduates of top-notch colleges who had majored in English, math, history, and science. But Levy's own vanity also factored into his embrace of Bernstein's idea. He was a career-changer himself—a Cornell graduate who had spent twenty years in the exclusive worlds of corporate law and finance before taking the helm of the nation's largest school system. He had started at one of the city's most competitive law firms, Skadden, Arps, Slate, Meagher & Flom, and worked his way up to director of global compliance at Citigroup, reporting directly to chairman Sanford Weill and making sure that employees in one hundred countries followed proper policies and laws. Although he had become involved in education through the Board of Regents, Levy saw himself as an outsider—a proud member of New York's cultural and corporate elite who could bring a fresh perspective to the school system and its problems. So did four of the seven members of the Board of Education, who had heeded Mayor Rudy Giuliani's pleas to hire a businessman this time instead of an educator, but had also defied him by choosing Levy, a self-described liberal who was close to some of the mayor's political enemies.

Around the country there was a rising clamor for non-educators to run beleaguered urban school systems, on the theory that they would be more willing than career educators to take risks, challenge the teachers' unions and other powerful interest groups with a stake in the status quo, and even experiment with private-sector strategies. This movement had its roots in 1983, when "A Nation At Risk," a report commissioned by the Reagan administration, warned that American schoolchildren had fallen scandalously behind their international peers, and business leaders began brainstorming for solutions. Nearly two decades later, one popular theory was that only a capitalist approach, with its emphasis on market competition and efficiency, could transform the insular, tradition-bound culture of school bureaucracies. Strangers to these systems would immediately spot and be outraged by nonsensical practices, the thinking went, while career educators would accept them as normal. In Chicago, for example, Paul Vallas, the city's former budget chief, had become schools chief and quickly ended automatic promotion from grade to grade, a practice that veteran educators defended as protecting students' self-esteem.

If businessmen could turn around school systems, Levy thought, why not also hire untraditional teachers, who might apply wisdom gleaned from other careers to the classroom in bold, creative ways? Why not plant as many Harold Levy prototypes as possible in schools desperate for innovation?

The timing was perfect: With the burgeoning standards movement, improving public education was now more of a national priority than it had been in decades. It was a focus of the presidential race between Al Gore and George W. Bush, who were both calling for people to drop other careers and become teachers. Moreover, the failure of urban schools was weighing on the nation's conscience during a time of almost unprecedented prosperity. A year-and-a-half before the terrorist attacks that would so powerfully alter the nation's confidence, Americans were enjoying an economic boom that had given many savings cushions seemingly overnight, and hence they were more open to taking chances with their careers.

It was a heady, indulgent time, and yet compared with their counterparts in the go-go '80s, beneficiaries of this boom were more concerned about social issues and more likely to complain of spiritual angst. Financial success and the comforts of yuppie life were not enough for many in this social stratum, of which

Harold Levy was a member. It was a demographic that Levy believed ripe for converting to the cause of urban education, which he and other civic-minded types were billing as the new civil rights movement—the biggest barrier keeping poor minorities from having the same opportunities as more affluent whites. A phrase from Abraham Lincoln's first inaugural address, when he predicted that "the better angels of our nature" would prevail in the Civil War and the two sides would reunite as one nation, stuck in Levy's mind as he fell hard for Bernstein's proposal.

"I want to make the New York City school system the employer of choice for the people who want to make a difference," he said in an interview with the *New York Times* that spring. "Whatever their background, this is a chance for them to dedicate their days to a cause that is larger, to something that gives a sense of purpose and satisfaction and wonderment at what humankind is capable of."

.   .   .

In mid-April, just a week after receiving Mills's threat, Levy told Vicki Bernstein to do whatever it took to get a career-changer program up and running by September. Besides the time table, the biggest hurdle was to convince New York State to allow a speeded-up certification process for such untraditional teachers. Given the looming crisis, however, Levy was confident that he could persuade Mills to recognize his recruits as certified if he could prove they were well-educated and committed.

For while both men believed certified teachers were generally far superior to their unlicensed counterparts, they were also among a growing group of leaders who thought traditional teacher preparation was deficient. Mills and the Board of Regents had already scratched the surface of this issue, changing the rules in 1999 so that all middle- and high-school teachers would have to major in the subjects they wanted to teach. The concern was that teacher preparation focused too much on amorphous education theory or child psychology, while neglecting the basic math, science, writing, and other skills that future teachers should know cold. New York was also acknowledging that education courses were not enough for would-be elementary school teachers, by requiring them to take a mix of liberal arts courses, too. Levy believed his career-changer program would appeal most to people with liberal arts educations, who could easily be brought up to speed on the pedagogical aspects of teaching that were now considered secondary, anyway.

One of Vicki Bernstein's first steps was to call the New Teacher Project, a three-year-old consulting firm that had spun off from Teach For America. That program, founded in 1991, recruited recent college graduates to spend two years teaching in poor urban and rural schools, and had set the precedent for luring bright idealists with no education background into the field. Now states and cities were hiring the firm to help recruit and train nontraditional teachers, using Teach For America's strategies. The firm, run by Teach For America alumni, helped school districts advertise for, interview, and train alternate-route teachers.

The recruitment strategy that Bernstein and the New Teacher Project conceived of was a clever blend of flattery and desperate appeal. Whoever signed up for the experiment would not be earning fat paychecks, after all, so the Board of Ed had to promise prestige of a different sort. The name of the program would be critical: To attract high-quality people, it had to sound prestigious, scholarly, selective—like a Rhodes scholarship, or a

Guggenheim fellowship. In a late-night brainstorming session, Michelle Rhee, the New Teacher Project's president, and Karla Oakley, a thirty-year-old Teach For America alumna in charge of launching the New York program, hit on New York City Teaching Fellows.

Even more important was the ad they created, a stroke of brilliance: At the top was a photo of a Hispanic girl, about nine years old, gazing sadly and squarely into the camera. Below were these words: Four out of five fourth-graders in our city's most challenged schools fail to meet state standards in reading and writing. Are you willing to do something about it?

Oakley showed a prototype to Bernstein one night at the Bryant Park Café, a trendy Manhattan restaurant, and they agreed it was perfect. They christened the ad "Sad Girl."

The old-timers who had overseen recruitment at the Board of Ed's human resources department for decades, and who liked to paint their school system as a happy realm of eager students, hated the ad. They thought it was terrible public relations to trumpet how many New York City children could not read at grade level. Who would want to teach in a system depicted so grimly, they asked? They wanted to ditch the sad girl for a smiling one. A less-discussed but equally valid question was how people who already taught in the school system would react to this ad, a blatant indictment of it. And how would their defensiveness and anger rebound to the do-gooders who joined the program?

But Levy overrode the naysayers and rushed the ad into print. It would appeal to just the kind of thoughtful, socially aware, risk-taking people he was looking for. The program would be expensive: Between the summer training, the graduate school tuition, and extra pay for teachers who would mentor the fellows, the Board of Ed would spend about $25,000 per fellow over two years, on top of their salaries.

"I did not want the kind of person who would teach because it's the safest alternative, the easiest thing to do," he said later. "These people would be doing it at a point of maturity in their lives where the choice is one that speaks to their mortality—to the question of 'What do I want to do with the rest of my life?'"

Just across the river from Levy's office in downtown Brooklyn, in her cool gray cubicle at Flemming, Zulack, Donna Moffett was asking herself just that sort of question.

.   .   .

That spring, Donna was planning a trip to London for her boss. The research took hours, but she did not find the work unpleasant. She had made friends with the concierge at Brown's Hotel and learned a lot about London. She had drawn up an hour-by-hour itinerary for Gerry Paul and his wife, with every address and phone number they could possibly need. On the first day of the trip, they would shop on Portobello Road and take a dinner cruise on the Thames. For later in the week, Donna had secured tickets to *Mamma Mia!* and *The Lion King*.

Such was Donna's life at Flemming, Zulack: quietly flipping switches for someone else's career. She had taken scrupulous care of Gerry Paul since 1991, when he had hired her on the recommendation of a mutual acquaintance. Her job included a great deal of typing—mostly client letters and billing statements, which she did at a whip-fast 100 words per minute. There were other workaday duties: answering Gerry's phone, making small talk with his clients, keeping track of checks and wire transfers. When out-of-town clients came to New York,

Donna made their hotel reservations, got them tables at desirable restaurants, and recommended museum exhibits. Because she was such a details person, she had also become the firm's events planner, hiring caterers, organizing menus, and ordering flowers for parties. Donna considered her salary a good one: $55,000 a year.

Donna laughed at Gerry's jokes, asked about his children, and traded recommendations with him on restaurants, movies, books, and CDs. She admired the family photos in his office while keeping the walls of her own cubicle nearly bare but for pictures of her baby niece, her younger sister's daughter. Gerry rarely asked about her life outside the firm, but she did not particularly mind; he was the one paying her, after all.

Donna's closest friend at the law firm was Peter Flemming, a white-haired, twinkle-eyed man who had been one of the founding partners. Peter had officially retired, but he still came in every few weeks to read his mail and visit Donna. Whenever he stopped by her cubicle, their conversation would quickly turn to subjects they both felt passionately about: poetry, politics, and, increasingly, urban education.

Peter had been a member of one of New York City's first community school boards in the early 1970s, and he had followed the politics and policies of the school system ever since, dashing off letters to officials and journalists at every chance. It was Peter who explained to Donna the tumultuous rise and fall of community control over the school system, one of the most divisive, perplexing chapters in the city's history.

The local school boards were created in 1969 in response to protests by blacks and Puerto Ricans in poor neighborhoods, who rightly believed their schools had been neglected by the white power base and wanted more control over them. Though

New York had made several attempts to integrate its schools after the *Brown v. Board of Education* decision in 1954, they failed due to opposition from whites and lack of interest from minorities, many of whom did not want their children attending schools outside their neighborhoods. Integration became an increasingly elusive goal through the '50s and '60s, since hundreds of thousands of middle-class whites were leaving for the suburbs and the school population, especially in Brooklyn and the Bronx, was becoming largely minority.

Despite this demographic shift, fewer than 10 percent of the city's teachers were black in the late '60s, another sore point for black parents. In Ocean Hill and Brownsville, Brooklyn, the neighborhoods that would become the epicenter of the community-control battles, the landscape was dominated by boarded-up storefronts and decaying tenements, and most of the residents were on welfare.

Though Peter had always embraced the community control experiment, others believed its good points were generally outweighed by the turmoil it brought about: The battle between the overwhelmingly white and Jewish teachers' union and militant blacks and Puerto Ricans in Ocean Hill–Brownsville, who tried to oust white and some black teachers from that neighborhood's mostly black schools using a blend of newly won community control and what many—though not Peter—perceived as racist and anti-Semitic scare tactics. The teachers' strike that followed, paralyzing the system in the fall of 1968. The corruption that for decades plagued some neighborhood school boards, some of whose members doled out school jobs to friends and family or used their seats as a springboard to higher office.

Peter was a hero to Donna for caring so passionately about inner-city schools, and over time, he opened her mind to the possibility of teaching. She showed him poems she'd written and confided some of the ideas she had for more fulfilling work: massage therapy, psychotherapy. A career aptitude test had supplied her with three options: teacher, lyricist, and poet. Peter joked that teachers and poets earned about the same piddling salary, but also reaffirmed his opinion that Donna would excel at whatever she chose to pursue. "What *can't* you do, Donna?" he would say.

No one else had ever talked to her that way, and she held onto his faith like a talisman.

·   ·   ·

Donna Moffett's own educational and professional background was a complex mix of hesitancy and adventurousness, false starts and dedicated perseverance. In Throgs Neck, the conservative, white, working-class section of the Bronx where she was raised, the public schools were indifferent at best, and Donna had gotten average grades with no effort. Her mother, a secretary, and stepfather, a middle manager, had never encouraged her to excel, or even to think about what would come after graduation. As long as Donna could type, her mother told her, she'd do just fine. She had briefly thought of becoming a stewardess, so that she could escape the Bronx and travel the world on airlines with glamorous names. But her stepfather had jeered—"You want to be serving other people's food your whole life?"—and Donna had put away the glossy airline brochures she had sent for.

When she graduated from Christopher Columbus High School on Astor Avenue and had to list a likely vocation in her yearbook, Donna put "teacher"—little knowing that three decades later, this casual prophecy would come to fruition.

Donna couldn't afford to go away to college, but on her own initiative she applied to Lehman College, a branch of the City University of New York that was three bus rides from her apartment building in the Bronx. A friend of hers was also enrolling, and had offered to drive Donna to campus every day. It was 1972, the height of the Vietnam era, and the intensity of the anti-war movement on campuses throughout the city might have been enough to unnerve a teenager who had seen so little of the world. Yet Donna had other, more immediate concerns. Living at home had become untenable because of family turmoil that, years later, she did not like to remember or discuss. So in the middle of her sophomore year, Donna dropped out of college and fled the Bronx, taking shelter with an aunt in upstate Orange County.

Ironically, although Donna's involuntary exile from New York was devastating for her formal education, in other ways it turned out to be tremendously liberating. Working as a receptionist when she was twenty, she met a friend with whom she moved to Cambridge, Massachusetts for a year. Donna found a job as a faculty secretary at Harvard's education school, where she assisted celebrated professors like Sarah Lawrence-Lightfoot and Joseph Featherstone. Then she moved to Chicago, where she took classes at the University of Chicago and helped run the city's first feminist bookshop, Jane Addams Book Store. When the bookstore did not bring in enough money to pay her rent, Donna went on to work as an administrative assistant for a nonprofit group that recruited lawyers for pro-bono work.

As Donna's social conscience developed, so did her interest in the arts: She began taking classes in quilt-making, silk-screening, and poetry. This intellectual and creative renaissance was what her education should have exposed her to, but hadn't. By the time she turned thirty-four, Donna had rejected nearly all the values held by the insular, conventional community in which she'd been raised. She had been liberated by the feminist movement and the arts, by literature and social justice projects; she was ready to return to New York.

.   .   .

Initially, the many small pleasures of her new life in her old city were enough to keep her satisfied. If she had left as a frightened girl from the Bronx, she returned as a Manhattanite— more confident, sophisticated, and socially aware. From that vantage point, New York had so much to offer. She moved into an apartment with a rooftop garden in Chelsea, and, still lacking a college degree, went to work for the New York County Bar Association. Two years later, she moved to Flemming, Zulack.

Eventually, though, Donna became restless and decided to return to school to complete her degree. She started taking early-morning and evening classes at Baruch College, one of the better branches of the City University of New York; by 1998 she had earned her bachelor's degree in English and won the college's top award for English majors. An extremely diligent student, Donna had nevertheless been surprised by her own success. When her professors and fellow students asked Donna what she wanted to do with her degree, teaching was one of the possibilities she always mentioned. But now that the possibility was becoming more real, Donna was torn. On one hand, it seemed too difficult a job, with the long hours and discipline issues and increasing expectations for what students needed to learn. On the other, it did not seem intellectually rigorous enough. Some of her Baruch professors had looked disdainful when she said she might become an elementary school teacher, suggesting it was a realm of underachievers. A few encouraged her to pursue a career in academia, but while she was honored that they would think her smart enough, Donna also considered her future pragmatically. She was in her mid-forties already, and despite her straight A's at Baruch, she did not think of herself as an intellectual. Teaching elementary school seemed much more within her grasp. But was she selling herself short? The debate dragged on in her mind.

Then, in 1999, Donna's doctor recommended that she have surgery due to a health problem that was deeply personal. The operation made Donna feel her mortality acutely, and she began to see her life in two phases: before surgery and after. She had let too many opportunities pass unexplored, as she kept her head down and let her simple job and comfortable salary carry her through the days and years like a sturdy but windowless train. It was time to decide how to spend phase two.

In the spring of 2000, encouraged by Peter Flemming, Donna enrolled in a graduate education course at Hunter College, another branch of CUNY. The course was called "The Art of Effective Teaching," and it perplexed Donna as much as it fascinated her. She and her classmates were a spirited bunch, and they had fierce debates about how to withstand the pressures of teaching as academic standards climbed ever higher and schools never had enough money or support.

Venturing into teaching during this era of increasing "accountability" for educators, to use the buzzword, seemed especially daunting to Donna. Rudy Giuliani, in his second term as mayor, had been bashing the city teachers' union for not allowing merit bonuses for teachers who excelled. Giuliani had also painted teachers as lazy, and said they deserved no salary raise unless they agreed to work longer hours. Meanwhile, Donna heard stories of city teachers who fled for the suburbs, fed up with the working conditions and the pitiful pay. While starting teacher salaries in most suburban districts were only a bit higher, the gap ballooned for more experienced teachers, who could earn tens of thousands of dollars more a year in places like Greenwich, Connecticut, and Ridgewood, New Jersey, than in New York.

She swung between thinking, "I have so much to give kids," and "I can't possibly give enough." The school system, with its 1,200 schools and infamous bureaucracy, overwhelmed her—some of her classmates had told her nightmarish stories about getting bounced around the hiring halls for hours and treated like dirt in the process—and she got a headache whenever she thought about seeking a job in it. Just as before, Donna was not systematically laying the path toward teaching—more thinking about it from a safe distance, even as she wrote long, ruminative papers for the Hunter class about what it meant to be a good teacher. Just as she had thought for years about volunteering with the homeless or the elderly, but ended up listening to stories about their plights on NPR rather than taking action.

But then, weeks after Donna's class ended, a friend she had met at Hunter called to ask if she had seen the newspaper ads about this new Teaching Fellows program. A lapsed Catholic, Donna did not believe in divine intervention. But when she checked out the ad, and then more detailed information on the Teaching Fellows Web site, the certainty that gripped her felt almost holy. She could get a master's degree in education without falling into debt. She could start training in a few weeks and teaching in September, with no time to procrastinate over her decision. Best of all, she could be part of a unique experiment, one elevated above the regular route to teaching by its purpose and the quality of people it drew. This last advantage was what drew Donna more than anything, because it addressed her deepest fears about teaching: that it was not an ambitious enough career, and that once in the system, she would have to face the pressures of teaching on her own, lost in a vast bureaucracy. "Join a network of outstanding individuals determined to make a difference," the ad said. The Teaching Fellows program offered not just a way in, but membership in an elite group of change-agents chosen by the system's top leadership.

The longing that rose in her shocked and thrilled her, and she almost did not think at all as she filled out the application. For once, she was letting emotion guide her and its intensity was druglike. This is it, she thought. This is what I've been waiting for. A path had been laid for her. Now she just had to prove she was worthy enough to follow it.

.   .   .

Donna Moffett's application was among more than 2,300 that landed at the Board of Ed's Brooklyn headquarters by late July. The applicants included lawyers, bankers, dot-commers, and social workers, a speechwriter for Rudy Giuliani, an acupuncturist, a judge, a hip-hop deejay, and a zookeeper. The average age was thirty-two, though 15 percent of the applicants were just out of college and some were in their fifties and sixties. About two-thirds were white, a striking contrast to the population of children they would be teaching.

Many of the aspiring fellows had held multiple jobs, which Vicki Bernstein and Karla Oakley considered a red flag. They had to wonder if the kind of person who would make this sud-

den leap into the unknown was really the bright, committed ide-
alist that Levy had envisioned. What if this first batch of teaching fellows turned out to be drifters and malcontents, unable to
stick to anything?

Bernstein and Oakley tried to weed out bad seeds during the
grueling six-hour interview sessions, in which each candidate
had to teach a five-minute sample lesson to a group of other applicants, discuss solutions to specific classroom problems posed
by interviewers, and sit for a one-on-one interview. Bernstein
learned to look for certain warning signs: Applicants who had
worked for the U.S. Census were suspect, for example, because
time and again, their résumés hinted they'd had a hard time
keeping a job for more than a few months. Also in the questionable category were people who had had their own cable-access
shows—surprisingly, there were several. Even more worrisome
were the Pollyanna candidates—people who seemed to expect to
change the world, or at least the lives of the children they
taught, overnight. How long would they last when confronted
with the realities of a crowded South Bronx classroom?

Overall, though, the people who made it to the interview
stage seemed smart, serious, and sincere about wanting to try
teaching. There were so many compelling applicants that the
Board of Ed ended up accepting 350, instead of the 250 it had
originally planned for. It finished hiring just a day before the
summer training began, with dozens of pieces yet to fall into
place.

Applicant Moffett was neither an obvious reject nor an obvious star. She could not brag of eye-catching accomplishments
like many others did: opera singer, chief surgeon, Marine, Wall
Street financier. Unlike many of her competitors, she had not
graduated from a prestigious college or worked with children in

day-care centers, homeless shelters, or after-school programs. Yet Donna's credentials were solid. She had been continuously employed since she was twenty. That she had earned her bachelor's degree only two years earlier, at forty-four, was more an asset than a liability, because it suggested determination and an ability to persevere. She had also already proved capable of working and attending school simultaneously. Her grade point average at Baruch was 3.79, well above the 3.0 the program required. And the screeners liked that she had taken a graduate-level education class, a sign that she was seriously interested in teaching and not just acting on a whim. On July 29, just a day after her interview, the Board of Ed called to tell Donna she was in.

She received the news as ecstatically as a high school senior getting a fat envelope from Harvard. Her boss, Gerry Paul, however, was floored. Did Donna have any idea what she was getting into? Gerry had taught in a city school himself for a brief period in the '70s, when the alternative was getting killed in Vietnam, and it had been no cakewalk. Relatives of his were career New York City teachers, and even now, years after their retirement, they complained about the system that had prematurely aged them.

And Donna, Gerry thought that morning after his prize secretary resigned, was not quite Parris Island material. Sure, she could handle whatever task he threw at her and charm clients and adversaries alike with her gentle humor and intelligence. But Donna Moffett in an inner-city school, with her own class of disadvantaged kids? Gerry had his doubts. When she formally gave notice, Gerry told her she could always come back if her new life didn't work out. He thought she needed to know that.

But while Donna was taking on more than she could know,

her leave-taking from Flemming, Zulack suggested as much as anything else why it was time for her to go. On the last Sunday in July, Donna packed her few personal belongings in a single box, sent her colleagues a formal-sounding farewell e-mail, and was gone. Even after ten years, her attachment to the place and her job was so tenuous that she could tiptoe out without so much as a backward glance.

.   .   .

The next day, Donna and the other 350 teaching fellows glimpsed each other for the first time in a welcoming ceremony at LaGuardia High School, just behind Lincoln Center. The day was exhilarating and nerve-wracking, fraught with the same heady anticipation that marked the college orientations they remembered from ten, fifteen, even thirty years earlier. The fellows wore stick-on nametags and carried thick folders of paperwork, subway maps, and schedules for the coming weeks of training. Banners that read "WELCOME TEACHING FELLOWS" hung everywhere, and journalists wended through the crowd, interviewing and photographing the inductees as if they were celebrities. At lunchtime, they sized one another up and traded reasons for enlisting, many of them sounding like religious converts.

Vicki Bernstein surveyed the group, trying to gauge by a show of hands how many were lawyers (a lot), were bilingual (many), had a doctorate (a handful), were taking pay cuts (almost all), had quit their job within the last week (at least half, Donna included), and were products of New York City schools (a surprising majority).

The tone was unabashedly inspirational. The dean of the education school at City University, where the fellows would get their master's degrees, invoked Christa McAuliffe and her motto: "I touch the future, I teach." Harold Levy addressed the crowd in his usual pinstriped suit, looking more like a banker than an education visionary. Many felt a kinship with this man, who they knew had abandoned his own job six months earlier because he wanted to do his part for urban education. They had read articles in the *Times* and other national newspapers about Levy's intention, as the first chancellor with a business background, to shake things up. They hoped—believed—that he saw them as special forces in that fight. Levy did not disappoint. The normally blunt chancellor's voice broke with emotion as he rallied the fellows and thanked them for accepting his challenge.

"The mountain you're about to climb is a very, very high mountain," he told his rapt audience. "I don't want to sugarcoat it. That's not fair to you and it's not fair to the people who you are going to serve. But on the other hand, what an opportunity! There is no child who can't make it. There is no child who is born unable."

This was the kind of rhetoric that had recently become fashionable during debates about the failures of urban education throughout the United States. "Every child can learn" was one of George W. Bush's mantras on the campaign trail, and the public went wild for it. Never mind how steep the odds might be for students who had been stunted by poverty and the teachers of varying ability who attempted to serve them. Levy's pronouncements sounded honorable, they sounded just, and the teaching fellows—whose ears still rang with the question, "Are you willing to do something about it?"—weren't about to pick them apart. Not yet.

"We can make urban education work," Levy went on, his

voice cresting. "I am convinced that urban education today has the same power, the same moral force, that the civil rights movement had in an earlier day, that the Peace Corps had in an earlier day. And where to do urban education more effectively than here?"

Then, a promise many of his anxious listeners seemed to stop breathing to catch every word of: "You're not in this alone," he said. "I'm not going to disappear. You're going to see lots of me. I want to understand what you encounter, people from the business world and academia. I want to understand how we can change this system, and I'm going to look to you to help me understand that . . . because you are the cutting edge, the shock troops, the people who are going to make this happen.

"Thank you for those children, as yet unchosen, who are about to be put in your charge," he finished, quiet now. "Thank you from the parents who often will not be able to articulate their gratitude. And thank you on behalf of the city."

The Fellows burst into applause, overcome by a sense of passionate purpose, like soldiers going to battle or missionaries to the South Seas. The atmosphere of collective determination and spirit was intoxicating. Donna Moffett, like so many of her new colleagues, was in tears. Here was just what she'd been seeking: a community with shared values and a mission so strong that they felt permanently bonded, even though they might remain strangers to one another.

There would be many days when, alone with twenty six-year-olds for hours on end, feeling cut off from the world in general and kindred spirits in particular, Donna would savor the memory of that moment.

CHAPTER THREE

Notwithstanding the tumble that had bruised her hip and her ego, Donna had savored her summer encounter with P.S. 92 and instinctively felt that the principal, Diana Rahmaan, would be a fine boss. Rahmaan, a black woman in her late forties who wore her hair in a dignified chignon, struck Donna as committed, kind, and inspiring when she invited the visiting fellows into her office during their visit and told them about her attempts to turn the school around. The walls had been painted a glaring, unsettling yellow when Rahmaan had arrived in August 1999, she'd told them, and packs of students had roamed the halls while teachers turned a blind eye.

Donna had handed Rahmaan her résumé as she was leaving that day, and had sought her out at the fellows' job fair the next week—even though they were supposed to let Vicki Bernstein's office assign them to schools. She saw P.S. 92 with the dreamiest of eyes—here was a school that had been governed by incompetence for years, it seemed, but now had been given a second chance—and was motivated by idealism and naiveté as she gently but persistently lobbied Rahmaan for a job.

Rahmaan, on the other hand, was motivated by desperation as she looked to fill five teaching vacancies in the weeks before school began. Rick Mills had followed through on his threat to sue the Board of Ed to stop the practice of hiring uncertified teachers in failing schools; a resulting court order required principals like Rahmaan to hire only certified teachers for the 2000–01 school year. Donna Moffett, for better or worse, fit the bill.

To be sure, Donna had no experience, and Rahmaan was understandably worried about how she would fare. But by the end of the summer, Donna would easily pass two of the three required state exams and complete enough hours of training to get "alternative certification," the new category that Mills and the Board of Regents had created just for the teaching fellows. To call them certified was almost laughable, since they had far less training and experience than many uncertified teachers, and only a sliver of the coursework required for traditional licensing. But Harold Levy had convinced the state that their status as "talented professionals" would make up for their gross deficiencies.

Diana Rahmaan could only hope he was right. She was taking a big chance with Donna, but she was working in a top-down system that gave her and other principals little choice in everything from the curriculum they used to the people they hired. About the fellows program, Rahmaan was guardedly optimistic. She herself had accepted a job at P.S. 92 the previous year because she believed an outsider's perspective was important—though not necessarily the crucial ingredient—in bringing about change. She hired not just Donna, but two other teaching fellows who had visited her school, hoping that their energy and enthusiasm would make up for all they surely did not know.

P.S. 92 had been on the state's list of failing schools since 1989, when the list was created to pressure consistently bad schools through public humiliation (it was released to newspapers), intensive monitoring, and the threat of closure if they did not improve. But even this punishment proved toothless at first, since the state and a series of chancellors remained powerless to intervene in how the failing schools were run. Instead, all decisions were left to the local school boards, which by law had sole power to hire and fire principals and other administrators, change curriculums, and experiment with other reforms.

Years of public outrage over patronage, educational failure, and outright corruption in some of the city's thirty-two community school districts had failed to produce change in Albany, since many New York City lawmakers had political ties to the local school boards. Many had gotten their political starts on the boards, and had filled them with cronies who would staff the district offices and schools with their friends and supporters.

But in 1996, after several well-publicized corruption scandals and intense lobbying by Rudy Giuliani and Rudy Crew, the popular new schools chancellor, the state legislature stripped the city's local school boards of most of their powers and gave them to the chancellor. Previous mayors and chancellors who tried to intervene in failing schools had usually been thwarted by defiant local boards, which went to court to stop them.

Around the time that the new law was passed, the State Education Department ordered Crew to step up pressure on several dozen failing schools, including P.S. 92. For the first time, a chancellor had the power to step in and enact sweeping changes in personnel and policy in individual schools, and the state wanted Crew to waste no time.

To back up its declaration that the schools were in dire straits, the state wrote up reports on all of them, detailing problems with leadership, curriculum, teachers, and facilities. The report on P.S. 92 found that the principal spent little time observing instruction in classrooms and quoted a teacher who claimed the principal was never available, except when "one of the teacher's classes had a riot." The report also found a haphazard approach to instruction, with "no continuity from one grade to the next" and no teacher training.

The student bathrooms at P.S. 92 lacked toilet seats and stall doors, according to the report, and the boys' bathroom stank of urine. Some classrooms were not in use "because of floors with missing tiles, leaking ceilings or falling paint chips." The report also noted "an accumulation of dirt" on staircases and in classrooms, and described roof repairs, which were being done the day of the visit, as potentially dangerous to students.

"Sparks from blowtorches could be seen coming down open shafts into classrooms," the report found. "Students, tables and chairs had to be moved to prevent fire."

Over the next three years, P.S. 92 had improved enough to avoid closing, a fate assigned to thirteen other schools in June 1999. But the school was still suffering; it had been through four principals in as many years, and the revolving-door leadership was clearly a huge liability. As part of a system-wide shakeup that June, Crew put P.S. 92 and forty-two other failing schools into an experimental "Chancellor's District," which he directly controlled. He replaced P.S. 92's latest principal with Diana Rahmaan, who had been a respected assistant principal at Prospect Heights High School, another troubled school about a mile away.

Crew also announced another, far more dramatic overhaul for P.S. 92 and all the others in the Chancellor's District. Under a deal he negotiated with the teachers' union, the schools would add forty minutes of instruction a day, along with five days for teacher training at the start of the school year. In exchange for the longer work schedule, teachers at these schools would receive a 15 percent raise, which meant the starting salary would be about $36,700 instead of $31,910.

Class sizes would be reduced to no more than twenty in kindergarten through third grade—a major difference from typical New York City classrooms, which had thirty-five, sometimes even forty, students. Some kindergarten and first-grade teachers would get aides like Ruth Baptiste, so that students could get more individual attention.

In the single biggest change, strict reading and math programs would be adopted at all elementary schools in the Chancellor's District, with reading lessons taking up the first ninety minutes of the school day and at least another forty-five in the afternoon.

A year later, Rudy Crew was out—the latest in a long line of chancellors to be driven from New York by political and ideological enemies. Harold Levy had become the school system's twelfth leader in two decades. The principals and teachers in the trenches had rolled their eyes and plodded on, knowing inconsistency was the only certainty at the Board of Ed. But Levy's lack of education expertise brought an unexpected benefit. Unlike the many chancellors who had come in with a whole new plan for the system, wanting to put their own stamp on it and create their own legacy, Levy would leave Crew's programs in place—for now, anyway. The Chancellor's District would remain intact, though whether or not it was a winning formula remained to be seen. It would take years to find out.

·   ·   ·

Donna almost immediately felt disillusioned with Success for All, the reading program that every teacher in the Chancellor's District had to use for the first ninety minutes of every day. The program is simple: It provides teachers with a literal script and down-to-the-minute schedule, breaking drill-like reading lessons into segments of no longer than ten minutes. The company also provides the reading material—for first-graders, a series of forty-five paperback storybooks, each stressing a different phonic sound.

Success for All schools conduct reading lessons in every classroom at the same time—first thing in the morning, when young children are most alert—grouping students by ability, not age. The groups are smaller than regular classes, with perhaps eight or ten students, so that the teacher can keep a close eye on each one's progress. For children still learning to read, the ninety-minute lessons involve chanting letters and small words in unison, to get used to their feel on the tongue.

To Donna's disappointment, most of her students were assigned to other classrooms for Success for All, because they had been grouped by ability. The students would be frequently tested and the groups reshuffled every eight weeks, but still, only about half of Donna's class would end up in her SFA group at some point during the year. For now, she had a group of mostly first- and second-graders from other classrooms, most of whom could not yet read.

Because it taught reading through phonics, which emphasizes sounding out letters and then words, Success for All was a lightning rod in the nation's so-called reading wars, which had long pitted conservatives against progressives in the education world's most politicized, bitter debate.

At heart the argument was more philosophical than pedagogical: Phonics represented discipline and order; whole language, freedom and creativity. Traditionalists—including the Christian Right, which embraced phonics instruction as part of its political platform—saw whole-language instruction as part of a permissive, loosey-goosey mentality that they believed was corrupting and weakening the nation. Progressive educators and their allies, on the other hand, saw the phonics approach as deadening, a threat to children's individuality and intellectual curiosity. More recently, phonics proponents had embraced the standardized-testing movement, saying that children must learn early that life is competitive, while the whole-language camp had opposed it on the grounds that test preparation is boring and takes time away from more stimulating lessons.

All through the twentieth century, the pendulum had swung between phonics, which emphasizes sounding out letters and words, and the whole-language method, which favors merely immersing children in good books and letting them figure out words from context. John Dewey was one of the early proponents of whole language. His progressive-education theory, embraced during the first half of the twentieth century, held that children learn best through hands-on experiences like paging through books or working on projects together, not drilling before a chalkboard. The most famous whole-language textbooks are the *Dick and Jane* series, which debuted in 1930 and were a fixture in public schools through the 1950s.

But with the cold war fear that American children were falling behind their international peers came a resistance to this "look-say" approach, as it was called then. In *Why Johnny Can't Read,* his best-selling 1955 book, Rudolf Flesch wrote that the method flew "in the face of all logic and common sense." He advocated a return to phonics, which had been used in the eighteenth and nineteenth centuries, and the nation listened.

The back-and-forth continued, cresting in California's embrace and then, when test scores fell, rejection of whole language in the late '80s and early '90s. But the battles were mostly local or of the ivory tower variety until the 2000 presidential campaign, when George W. Bush, who had introduced impressive-looking education reforms as the governor of Texas, advocated phonics as the superior method of teaching reading. His position had won him points with the Christian and conservative wings of the Republican Party in Texas, and it would again in the presidential election.

When Bush became president in January 2001, it would take him less than a month to push through his No Child Left Behind Act, bringing sweeping changes in education policy that included a required emphasis on phonics. To qualify for federal reading funds, school districts would have to use "scientifically grounded" programs, covering five principles that research favored by Mr. Bush deemed critical: phonemic awareness, fluency, vocabulary, comprehension, and phonics. The Bush administration would claim not to advocate particular programs. But as it happened, only a few would meet the criteria of the new law, all of which had systematic phonics instruction as their centerpiece. So when states applied for the grant money, many would promise to use these programs.

But before Bush even ran for president, New York City had invested heavily in one of the programs, Success for All.

Success for All was about as business-like, bottom line–driven an approach to reading instruction as existed, the goal being to raise reading test scores. Its defenders lambasted whole-language programs as liberal fads that foolishly promoted creativity over no-nonsense acquisition of basic skills. While many white, middle-class schools still embraced less rigid approaches, failing inner-city schools no longer had the choice.

Robert Slavin, a researcher at Johns Hopkins University, had developed Success for All in the 1980s on the theory that structure, rules, and consistency were what disadvantaged children needed to learn to read, with every classroom in a school using the same instructional techniques simultaneously. Success for All was tested in a handful of Baltimore schools in the late 1980s and then in Philadelphia, with promising results. By 1999, when Rudy Crew ordered P.S. 92 and the other schools in the Chancellor's District to adopt Success for All, it had become one of the most popular programs in the country for improving troubled schools. About 1,500 schools around the country had bought into Success for All by 2000, at the cost of $60 million a year.

Large school systems like New York's were drawn to Success for All because it provided a uniform way of doing things—from the materials down to the script and even special hand signals that teachers use to keep students' attention and praise them. In the past, low-performing schools, including P.S. 92, tended to try several reading programs at once, so that a student might be steeped in one method in third grade, then be subjected to an entirely different program in fourth. With all the variation, it was impossible to measure a school's progress from one year to the next, let alone an individual child's. With every class in a school using Success for All, Rudy Crew hoped, teachers would be more effective, students would learn to read faster, and progress could be measured more smoothly.

The prepackaged lessons were supposed to ensure that all teachers—even novices and the laziest or most inept veterans—

could teach reading. All they have to do, theoretically, is read the script. In placing Donna and the other teaching fellows in schools that used Success for All, the Board of Ed hoped it was all but guaranteeing their success with reading instruction, since the program would guide them every step of the way. The fellows, like all teachers new to Success for All, got two days of training in August, were handed fat teachers' guides, and were essentially told, "Here are your lines."

Donna was disappointed because she had thought a lot about how she would teach reading, and felt eminently more qualified to teach it than math and other subjects. She had won Baruch's literature prize, after all, and had devoured books all her life, starting with *Harold and the Purple Crayon* at the Throgs Neck branch of the New York Public Library. She had bought several dozen storybooks for her classroom, including some, like *Jamberry*, that her niece loved. She had pictured reading stories of her own choosing to the students several times a day, a ritual she believed would infuse them with joy and imaginative spirit, so that they would see reading as the treat that it was and find the will to do it on their own.

Although the Board of Ed had presented Success for All as a godsend during the fellows' summer training, many encountered a far less rosy attitude toward the program when they arrived on the job. Some teachers at Donna's school called it "Stress for All" and grumbled about how their classes might as well be taught by robots, since it prevented them from bringing their own style and ideas to reading instruction.

While veterans said they could teach Success for All on autopilot, Donna struggled to learn its rhythms. For the first few months, it felt like rubbing her stomach, patting her head, and tapping her foot all at once as she tried to read the script aloud while reading the italicized teachers' instructions to herself and using the Success for All hand signals. To command total silence, for example, she was supposed to raise her right hand over her head in a "stop" gesture. For "active listening"—sitting still with folded hands and eyes on the teacher—she had to make a V with her index and middle fingers. There were also goofy catchphrases: telling the students to "buddy buzz" when it was time to read to one another, and to "think, pair, share" when she asked questions about a story.

Donna disliked the repetition involved—how a class had to stay on the same letter and same story, written by Success for All people and not very inspiring, for days at a time. She got bored fast, and she could tell that many of the students did, too. The stories were paired with "authentic literature," as it is known in the education world—tales by Ezra Jack Keats, Vera B. Williams, and other respected children's authors, which Donna admired. But there was no time to savor these stories, to linger over delicious words and phrases as she had done in early September with *Jamberry*. Often, with the brief time allotted, Donna did not even make it through the "authentic literature" selection.

The children seemed not only bored by Success for All, but made nervous by the rigid schedule. Some, like Stefanie, hated leaving their classroom shortly after arriving in the morning to go to their SFA groups. When the SFA music came over the PA system at 8:45 sharp, things got chaotic as the school's 1,100 students, in a Pavlovian response, leapt from their seats and scurried through the halls to their groups. When Donna's students returned to Room 218, they were often so wound up after sitting and drilling for ninety minutes that she could not get them to line up quietly for lunch. Stress for All, indeed.

Yet the program already appeared to be living up to its name at P.S. 92—in its first year, 1999–2000, reading scores had risen by several percentage points, enough for the school to finally come off the state's "failing" list. But because of the school's long history of problems, and because it was typical for test scores to jump in the first year of any new program, nobody was celebrating just yet. Success for All had to be strictly adhered to, and the ninety minutes devoted to it could never under any circumstances be used for another purpose—not even to read a good book. Every child's future depended on it, Diana Rahmaan told her staff in a meeting the first week of school, as did P.S. 92's.

. . . .

Despite the strictures of Success for All, exhilaration swelled inside Donna time and again in the first month of school, sometimes spilling out in spontaneous laughter that was one of her signature traits. At those moments, Donna seemed to her students like a cartoon character come to life, a playmate whose whimsy and enthusiasm put her in an entirely different category from the frowning teachers they glimpsed in the halls. After a few weeks of feeling uncomfortable in her law-firm outfits—they felt out of place in a first-grade classroom, and besides, they had never suited her personality—Donna took to wearing loose, colorful dresses and dangly necklaces and earrings that she hoped would delight the children, including a pair shaped like sushi rolls.

She taught the class one of her favorite songs from childhood, "The Good Ship Lollipop," and when they sang it some mornings—even Curtis joined in, after copious eye-rolling—students who happened to be passing by would pop their heads in and stare at this teacher who was acting silly in a pla⟨e⟩ seriousness reigned.

When a student answered a question correctly, Donna would bound over and pump her hand, saying "All right, girl! Excellent!" while the child beamed and the others stared in delight.

After school, on these exuberant days, Donna hummed with energy as she stapled even the most crudely lettered worksheets to the walls—a practice she would soon learn was unacceptable, since the school wanted only exemplary work on display, so-called proof that it was on the upswing—rearranged her book shelves, or graded homework with a purple pen. Her heart thumped purposefully as the janitors whistled in the halls and the golden autumn light faded. "I feel so alive!" she would marvel.

Donna's relationships with the students deepened as she learned each one's habits and quirks, weaknesses and strengths. When she was away from them, late at night or on weekends, their expressions and remarks floated through her mind. A few of the students had begun calling her Miss Muffin, which she loved but pretended not to, mock-scolding, "I am your teacher, not a breakfast food!" As she discovered their fears, senses of humor, and even the treasures they stowed in their pockets—for serious Jamilla, a tiny notebook she called her journal; for a too-cool girl named Tasha, a plastic cell phone—she developed a loyalty toward them that grew fiercer by the day. They seemed to sense it, showing their appreciation in small ways. One day, as she read to them in the story corner, she felt something glide over her foot and glanced down to see Stefanie tenderly stroking her shoe.

Nicole Peat, the birdlike girl whose uniform was too big, had scrambled in one morning, tugged at Donna's sleeve, and whis-

pered, "Ms. Moffett, I had a dream about you! I dreamed me
and you went on a plane together to somewhere far away."

.   .   .

Yet Donna was also coming to terms with the reality that lay
beyond her first adrenaline-fueled weeks in Room 218. As Indian summer ran out and cooler, sharper October got underway,
her jubilant moments were increasingly eclipsed by darker ones,
when her new job felt like a test that she was quickly and spec-
tacularly failing. The physical adjustments alone were overwhelming: Donna's back throbbed from standing all day, her
eyes ached from constantly scanning her classroom, and her
throat was raw. She had thoroughly exhausted her vocal cords by
October, and not just from talking for hours on end. She had
traded her gentle manner of speaking for a louder, harsher tone,
the better to reach twenty sets of small ears and make clear that
Ms. Moffett meant business.

Donna had to reinforce that message with her whole being,
squaring her shoulders, thrusting out her chin, narrowing her
eyes into slits, folding her arms, and leaning against the wall like
a sheriff. Once her body was positioned, she would clench the
muscles in her throat and spit out words with as much force as
she could muster. Even at normal volume, the effort to project
her voice, actress-like, around the large classroom shocked her
system.

One of the biggest threats to her sense of competence was
Christopher Samms, a boy so small he could have passed for a
pre-kindergarten student. Christopher's eyes and mind were always racing, his spindly arms casting about, and he was determined not to let ten minutes pass without making his presence

known. His favorite trick was tipping his chair over, then scooting on his belly across the floor, under other children's desks. When Donna scolded him, he blinked vacantly or looked past her, seeking a new way to misbehave.

Christopher infuriated her, yet at times he seemed painfully vulnerable. One day in art class, when all the other students drew happy jack-o'-lanterns, Christopher drew one with huge tears under its triangle eyes. Donna wrote to his mother, asking her to come for a conference the next morning. But she did not show up, and Christopher arrived almost two hours late that day.

If Donna's struggles with Christopher were her first evidence that parents would disappoint her, her problems with Luis Sanchez, the boy who would not stay in his seat the first few weeks of school, foretold that her superiors would fail to explain decisions that deeply affected her or her students, much less bring Donna in on them. During lessons, Luis would inevitably run to Donna's desk and rummage through the drawers or just jog around the room, grunting. One morning he climbed onto the windowsill and announced he would jump out—an idle threat, since the lower windows were sealed shut, but one that left Donna hyperventilating. When she complained, Brenda Robertson told her that Luis would soon be transferred to a special-education program for students who could not function in a normal classroom.

Donna silently fumed, but was too polite to ask why she, a novice completely unequipped to handle a child like Luis, had been stuck with him. She had little sympathy for Luis; instead, she resented him for creating so much mayhem in her classroom, which she wanted to be a peaceful, happy kingdom.

Perhaps the biggest problem Donna faced was Cynthia Alvarez, a Puerto Rican girl who had not enrolled in school until late September. Cindy screamed hysterically if her mother left her side, so the school allowed the woman to sit in Donna's classroom for two weeks, whispering to Cindy in Spanish. After the mother stopped coming to class, Cindy would sometimes cry all day, breaking only for lunch.

She looked adorable, with short, shaggy black hair and huge brown eyes. But several times already, she had stolen other children's pencils or snacks. When she wasn't crying, she was often hitting or saying bad words when Donna's back was turned.

"Ms. Moffett, she called me dickhead!" Curtis said one day as he stood in line next to Cindy.

"She shoved me and said the F-word and 'bitch'," Stefanie reported, clutching her arm and grimacing.

Since Cindy's mother spoke no English and Donna knew only a few words of Spanish, they had barely communicated. But other teachers had passed on troubling information: Cindy had started kindergarten the previous year, they told Donna, but would get so hysterical when her mother left that the mother withdrew her.

Donna was amazed that the school system had let Cindy drop out, but in fact, kindergarten is not mandatory in New York. Not only is it fine for a child to show up in first grade with no previous schooling, but the system does not have to provide extra help, like tutoring or counseling. And Donna, looking at this volatile, blank-faced girl who wrote nothing in her notebook, had no clue how to begin. This was her first hint of the emptiness behind the "every child can learn" rhetoric—the hard, cold, shocking fact that it was entirely up to her to get a child like Cindy up to speed.

.   .   .

As Donna grappled with her problem students, the vibe from the school administration began to change. It had been politely welcoming for the first few weeks, but no longer. Diana Rahmaan had visited Donna's classroom only once, and Donna had yet to have a substantive conversation with this woman whose personality and vision had drawn her to P.S. 92. Rahmaan, she was learning, was far too busy with the broad aspects of running a huge school—paperwork, administrative meetings, student discipline, budgeting—to advise and support Donna. In a school the size of P.S. 92, such supervisory tasks were delegated to the assistant principals, like Brenda Robertson. And just as Donna had resorted to intimidating postures and tones to let the students know school was not a game, Robertson—a very different personality from Rahmaan—was doing the same with her.

But Robertson, a tall black woman who could win the fiercest staring contest, was much more naturally strict. She stopped by Donna's classroom once or twice a day, and had been taking it upon herself to intervene when Donna was trying to get her class under control. Robertson had been a teacher for years, and clearly prided herself on her disciplinary skills. Early on, she had told Donna that she could tame even the wildest class in two weeks.

Sure enough, no matter how many of Donna's students were chattering or jumping from their seats, all fell silent when Robertson strode in, arched her brows, and fixed them with a steely gaze. She had to utter only three words in her sharp voice—"*Boys* and *girls*"—to get them sitting up straight. She sometimes gave Donna the same look, and Donna would feel as cowed as the students until Robertson turned and strode out.

She sometimes allowed a tight-lipped smile when Donna engaged the students in humorous small talk or looked up from a story to seek their feedback. Mostly, though, Robertson leaned against the chalkboard or paced around the room with folded arms, almost never offering a compliment or murmur of approval. When she did speak up, it was often to point out problems with the classroom layout, the wall hangings, and Donna's discipline skills, or "classroom management" in Board of Ed lingo. Donna had arranged the desks in a horseshoe shape, with each facing front; Robertson made her rearrange them into clusters so students could team up for reading and writing projects. Donna wanted to hang student drawings and her photos of them and their parents; Robertson insisted that she hang only student work that jibed with the lesson plans and write at the bottom of each sample which instructional standard it met, as evidence for visitors that the school was following state requirements.

Robertson paid little notice to the quirky classroom decorations, whimsical storybooks, and other materials that Donna had painstakingly chosen, like the park ranger's badge and bug kit. She insisted that the Edna St. Vincent Millay and Langston Hughes poems come off the wall—they were "age inappropriate," she said.

Donna wanted so much to win Robertson's respect, just as she had sought to impress Gerry at the law firm. Gerry had always been appreciative, showering her with thanks when she finished a typing project ahead of schedule or lavished attention on an out-of-town client. Between his praise and his frequent quips that she was too smart to be a secretary, Gerry had always made her feel competent and valued.

At P.S. 92, it was just the opposite—Donna was starving for even a scrap of encouragement. She wished her new colleagues would acknowledge how much she had given up to become a teacher more than halfway through her life, or compliment her efforts. But this world she had entered didn't operate that way. Its culture and language were completely foreign, and her initial attempts to penetrate them failed. The tools Donna had used to ensure good relationships at the law firm—sincere praise, disarming small talk, and a cheerful attitude—were no longer failsafe. When Donna complimented Brenda Robertson's outfit or the way she led a meeting, Robertson responded coolly, with a clipped, "Thank you, Ms. Moffett." When Robertson swept into the classroom and Donna stopped whatever activity was underway to have the class trill, "Good *morning*, Ms. Robertson," the response was similarly terse. Perhaps Robertson thought it premature to compliment Donna when her weaknesses were still so glaring, for fear it would make her complacent.

She used to care for one man and bask in his praise. Now she cared for twenty children, the most emotionally draining experience of her life, yet felt almost wholly deprived of encouragement.

·   ·   ·

Between the discipline problems and the rigidity of the P.S. 92 schedule, Donna felt caught in a vice that was tightening by the day. One Friday morning in October, she hunkered down in the story corner with her Success for All group, conducting a lesson that starred the letter *K*. She pointed to a cardboard *K* on the wall with "Ms. Moffett's magic wand": a pink plastic rod with silver fringe, which she had bought to replace the standard pointer that came with her Success for All materials. "Boys and girls, what is this letter? Are we ready to trace this letter with our magic pencils?"

Then came the drill: "Stroke down, lift, kick in, kick out!

Stroke down, lift, kick in, kick out!" The students chanted with her, tracing imaginary *K*s with "magic pencils"—their fingers. Then, a glance at the Success for All manual in her lap and on to the next chant: "The sound of *K* is K-K-K-K-K!"

Next, a game of "Say, Spell, Say": chanting, then spelling words that contain *K* and that had appeared in a Success for All story, "Kim's Visit." They clapped in time with the letters, making the lesson sound all the more like a military drill.

"Asks," the students chanted, staring blankly at Donna or the floor. "A-S-K-S. Asks. Kit. K-I-T. Kit. Packs. P-A-C-K-S. Packs. Sick. S-I-C-K. Sick."

Right on time, Donna began another game, asking individual students to come up with words that started with *K*. Nicole, who was always engaged, impressed Donna by offering, "Kangaroo!" Donna nodded and raised her eyebrows before moving on to a boy named Shane, who shouted, "King!" When it was Curtis's turn, he paused, then tentatively said, "Curls?"

"'Curls' is a good guess, but that starts with the letter *C*," Donna said. Stefanie, who could not wait another second for her turn, shouted, "Kitten!" "Very good, Stefanie," Donna said, "but there's no calling out."

At 9:30, she sent the students back to their seats to work on what amounted to an art project: a Success for All worksheet sprinkled with letters and a kite, which they were supposed to color, then cut out with scissors. They colored happily but, as it turned out, too quickly. Most were finished by 9:45, a full half-hour before lunch. As a few children collected the art supplies and put them away, the rest started fiddling in their desks and chattering, ignoring Donna's "zero noise" hand signal. The muscles around her jaw tightened; she was losing control of her classroom, but this time, anger crowded out the usual humiliation and self-reproach. This time, instead of blaming herself, Donna faulted them for not caring about their own education. Frustration overpowered the sense of decorum that had guided her every move in the workplace for decades, and she melted down.

"WHAT IS GOING ON HERE?" she shouted, loud enough for neighboring classrooms to hear. This immediately captured the children's attention. While she had it, Donna announced that there was enough time for another activity: reading stories out loud from the Success for All "blue books." There was, however, a problem: Donna had sent the blue books home with the students the previous night, and hardly any had brought them back. Donna, still furious, lashed out again:

"Your blue book is always with you!" she hollered. "That's it! That's the rule!"

With twenty minutes until lunch, she made the class recite the rule about blue books: "They go home with you, they come back with you. They go home with you, they come back with you." Then she congratulated the two students who did remember the books, Tasha and Manette, the girl who always wore a lacy white headscarf in accordance with her family's Pentecostal religion. Manette was usually a space cadet, staring around the room with bug eyes and always asking Donna to repeat questions. Exhausted and suddenly aware that she was shaking with hunger, Donna pulled two brand-new storybooks from her desk to reward the girls and retreated to her desk, where a cold cup of coffee, a bagel, and two cookies from the teachers' lounge sat untouched.

Donna asked the class to be quiet while she wrote small notes in the front of each book. But of course, they were anything but silent as she sat at her desk to inscribe the gifts and collect her or, the rumpled boy who sometimes wore pajama tops to school, led the follies that ensued. He acted younger than six, often prattling like a toddler and shuffling around the room without lifting his feet from the floor. Academically, he seemed almost as clueless as Christopher, his partner in crime. As Donna caught her breath, Trevor spread his fingers over his face, hooted loudly like an owl, and began scooting around the room in his chair, its wooden legs squeaking against the floor. Christopher followed close behind, hooting, too, and looking wildly around the room to see who was watching.

At 10:00, Donna passed out reward stickers for the third time that morning, since they were the only thing that got everybody to shut up. She put some stickers on outstretched wrists; others she stuck on foreheads, commanding the puzzled students, "Do not remove it from where I put it." It was a last-ditch effort to exert control over children who had been skillfully controlling her all morning.

Only ten minutes of Success for All remained when she finally passed out spare blue books and began reading aloud, asking the students to follow with their fingers. They were only on page 6 when classical music piped through the public address system, signaling the end of Success for All. The children had finally grown silent and were fully absorbed in the story, but it was time to quit.

. . .

As much as she resented SFA, Donna had even more difficulty with the other four hours of the school day, when there were just as many standards to meet but no script to guide her. She was supposed to teach math five days a week, social studies three, and science two; one of the remaining afternoon periods was devoted to more reading, the other to elective subjects—art, dance, computers, and music—taught by other teachers while Donna had her prep period. A poster taped to her blackboard charted out the schedule in bold magic marker. But after lunch, the minutes slipped through Donna's fingers like weightless little beads and she struggled mightily to use the time the way she was expected to.

The problem was aggravated by the behavior of children like Cindy and Christopher, which slowed her down even on a good day and ground things to a halt on days when she was already having a hard time with lessons. Donna began keeping a daily log of misbehavior, a symbol of her isolation and growing anger, which typically went something like this: *Christopher will not sit, constantly out of seat, goes in closet, crawls around. Tasha humming, sticking tape on her head. Cindy keeps jacket on, cries when Mom leaves. Briella hits self in head. Curtis calls out inappropriate comments and uses profane language. Stefanie rocks back in chair, tips chair over, screams, takes things and will not return them. Christopher crawls under teacher's and students' desks, does not follow directions, inappropriate comments.*

One morning, several students kept whispering as Donna brought the class upstairs from the cafeteria. Each time they did, she stopped the line and held up her hand to order silence. Walk, whisper, stop. Walk, whisper, stop. It took nearly fifteen minutes to get upstairs.

The math lesson should have started at 11:06, and when Brenda Robertson spied the class returning from the bathroom at 11:25, she looked livid. No matter how badly Donna's students were behaving, she had no excuse for falling this far behind schedule.

Every period in the school day had been carefully planned, so that every student would have a set amount of time reading, writing, and doing math. There was not a minute to spare. This was exactly the kind of scene that the people from the district office and the state would seize on as evidence that P.S. 92 was not on top of its game.

Robertson was waiting at the door of Room 218 when Donna and her class finally arrived, and her expression was searing.

"Ms. Moffett, may I have a word?"

Donna's mouth and eyes, which had smiled eagerly when she saw Robertson, hardened as the students filed into the classroom and she waited for the rebuke. Her upbringing as a teacher, with all its rigidity and unimaginativeness, was perhaps stirring memories of her upbringing as a child in the Bronx, and triggering a rebellious reaction.

"Yes, Ms. Robertson?"

"I find this unacceptable," Robertson told her in a low, firm voice, her eyes fixed on Donna's. "You have to get these students back to your classroom on time just like the rest of the teachers in this school. I can't afford to have you roaming the halls with them when you're supposed to be teaching them math."

Donna's face burned as if she had been slapped. Her eyes darted to the classroom, and saw some of the students peering curiously her way.

"I'm so sorry, Ms. Robertson," she said. "It won't happen again."

"I hope not," the assistant principal said, letting her eyes rest on Donna for another few seconds before she turned away.

Back in the classroom, Donna hurriedly wrote the "learning objective" on the board: *Students will compare links to other objects*, meant to get the children thinking about the concepts of size and measurement. Increasingly at struggling schools around the country, teachers were required to post a learning objective before every lesson, to remind themselves, their students, and any visitors what curriculum standard the lesson met. Never mind that most of Donna's students couldn't yet read the simplest sentences—as long as she was following the protocol handed down by the central administration, and posting so-called evidence that she and her students were following the program, they would be left all too alone for now.

She gave each student "manipulatives"—jargon for small pieces of plastic or wood that can be counted or measured as part of math class. Then she asked them to determine which of their manipulatives was longest. "I want everybody to think about whether your rod is shorter, longer, or the same size as your link," she announced. The students were thrilled to be presented with smooth, brightly colored pieces of plastic that looked like toys. Trevor and Christopher started sword-fighting while the others at their table looked on.

"Whose rod is shorter?" Donna intervened, taking one boy's hand in each of hers and making them hold up their rods. "S-H-O-R-T-E-R," she ad-libbed. "Class, repeat after me." They did.

Since they seemed to like the rods better than the links, she tried to keep their interest by having several students at a time hold up their rods and have the class vote on whose was longest. She gave each student a third kind of manipulative, a plastic gingerbread man, but that only made things more chaotic. By 11:55, she was not sure what to do next, even though math class had started twenty minutes later than it should have.

"My links are longer than my rods," she said hopefully, holding the two shapes against the blackboard. When Luis started whipping his gingerbread man with his rod, she took it as a cue to collect the manipulatives and stash them out of sight. Though Donna had followed the lesson plan provided by the math-program company, the lesson had been a failure because she had not organized carefully enough and because her students could not sit still.

"Maybe we have to do math differently," Donna said as the students reluctantly dropped their playthings into a basket. "Maybe we have to do math without these wonderful manipulatives that everyone loves so much."

·   ·   ·

Brenda Robertson was taking note of the frequent disarray in Room 218, and her patience, like that of many assistant principals supervising teaching fellows that fall, appeared to be running out. One afternoon when she walked in to find Donna reading a story to her class during the math period, her frustration boiled over. After all, if Donna Moffett failed, it would be Robertson's failure, too.

The teaching fellows were getting all kinds of attention, and Chancellor Levy had commanded principals and assistant principals to go out of their way to support them. Never mind that most of these supervisors had learned their craft the hard way: putting themselves through school, student-teaching, and spending years in difficult classrooms before getting a title that was even remotely prestigious. To many, the teaching fellows seemed like another breed altogether—smug, entitled, thinking they were New York's version of Mother Teresa, blessing the schools with their presence and their Newbery Award books. As if that was all teaching was, many assistant principals huffed to themselves and their confidants that fall.

Robertson seemed turned off by Donna's attitude—the smile forever on her face and the flattery she spouted, as if that would excuse the disarray in her classroom. One afternoon in mid-October, she summoned Donna to her office after school and let her have it. Didn't she understand the high stakes? Public School 92 would not tolerate a teacher who flouted the rules, she told Donna—especially a new teacher who didn't know what she was doing.

"This is *unacceptable*," Donna later recalled Robertson saying. "I cannot afford to lose these children."

But at that moment, something shifted in Donna: Instead of apologizing, she wanted, needed, to show she would not be intimidated. She returned Robertson's stare, trying to keep her voice from shaking, and said, "This will not be an abusive relationship."

The staring match continued.

For the first time, Donna considered walking out of P.S. 92 and never coming back.

.　　.　　.

The confrontation, though brief, led to the physical and emotional crisis of Donna's first term. Days later, on October 15, her voice collapsed into a pitiful croak and she developed a respiratory infection. She missed school for five days, using all but three of her sick days for the entire year. Nursing her aching throat and lungs in her cozy, daintily decorated apartment, she wept and briefly let herself imagine not returning to P.S. 92. She longed to feel appreciated, but instead she felt despised. She veered between self-pity and outrage as she replayed the showdown with Robertson and the tensions that had led up to it.

Maybe she really was a failure and should not be teaching children. Or maybe, she thought miserably, Robertson and others at P.S. 92 merely hated her status as a teaching fellow.

The dispiriting chaos at P.S. 92, the endless exhaustion and numbing humiliations had knocked Donna flat. She knew she had to conquer all of it, and feared she couldn't. Here she was, finally doing something she felt passionate about, yet she was proving unequipped for the job to which she had fused her identity.

Failing as a teacher was not an option for Donna—the disappointment would be impossible to bear. With the stakes so high, her only choice was to attack each day in a frenzy. But her body, vulnerable despite her boldness of spirit, seemed barely able to handle the strain.

Ironically, the full force of Donna's isolation hit her after a visit from her deputy superintendent in late October. Though her voice was still wounded and raspy, she had been in a good mood that morning as the students settled into their seats. "Raise your hand if you know what day it is," Donna said, following the routine she had established to get them alert. Curtis was among the few to thrust out an arm, and she called on him, eager to take advantage of his rare enthusiasm.

"Today is October," he announced with authority. Instead of moaning under her breath, Donna suppressed a cheer. It was so unusual for Curtis to participate—happily, no less—that his blooper sounded as sweet as the right answer. She assured him that he was partly right, then let Shakeela, who was turning out to be the class prodigy, fill in the rest.

When Donna asked what holiday would be celebrated the following week, Curtis's hand shot up again, and he deliberately kept his lips sealed as several students violated the rules by whispering. Donna wrote his name on the board to note his good behavior, a practice she had begun several weeks earlier to reward silence, sharing, and other good behavior. Students who made the list got checks next to their names for each new show of good habits. Those with the most checks at the end of the day got a reward: a sparkly sticker, maybe, or a super ball. So far, it was working much better than other experiments that Donna had tried, like promises of parties, which drew the ire of the administration, or her attempts to make Luis and Stefanie the teacher when they were running around the room.

The morning was proceeding with unusual smoothness when there was a terse knock and in walked Irwin Kurz, the superintendent who supervised P.S. 92 and all of the other Brooklyn schools in the Chancellor's District. Kurz, who wore suits every day and was entering his fourth decade in the school system, was genuinely excited about the several dozen teaching fellows in his schools. He thought they seemed more motivated, and in many cases smarter, than the teachers who entered through the traditional route. He had heard that Donna had been out sick, and he wanted to buck her up with a visit. But like a presidential stopover in a third-world country, it was purely symbolic—Kurz was not about to take off his suit jacket and demonstrate how to teach.

"I came to tell you how good you're doing," Kurz told the students, who had fallen silent and were gazing at him with curiosity and shyness. "You're doing very, very nicely."

Trevor twisted around to shoot Christopher a look. "Excuse me, can you face me please?" Kurz called out as Donna hustled over to straighten Trevor out. "What's your favorite subject?" he persisted, trying to keep their attention. The answers poured forth with no regard for Donna's hand-raising rule: McDonald's. Basketball. Computers. Curtis, whose face had twisted into its usual grimace when Kurz took over, raised his hand, and Kurz eagerly called on him. "I like blood from *Scream*," he offered, referring to the popular teen-slasher movie. Kurz nodded, but his grin was replaced with a look of consternation and he moved toward the door. He waved goodbye and urged the children to stay on their best behavior. Suddenly, Curtis blurted out: "Goodbye, Mr. Scary Movie!" The class erupted in laughter, and the progress that Donna had reason to hope for minutes earlier now seemed out of the question. It was 8:25 a.m.

. . .

As Kurz hurried out of Room 218 that day, on to his real job of supervising adults, Donna realized how isolated she felt—what had been in that visit for her, anyway? Her new job was surprisingly lonely and, though she didn't like to admit it, disappointingly mundane. As a secretary at Harvard and later for assorted lawyers, she was constantly on the phone or in meetings with smart, sophisticated professionals. At Flemming, Zulack she sat close enough to another lawyer's secretary to chat throughout the day if she wanted to.

But at P.S. 92, Donna spent most of her workday behind the closed door of her classroom, the only adult among twenty children who still had their baby teeth. Confronted with their stale morning breath, perpetually sticky hands, sniffles and coughs and high-pitched demands, it was easy to long for a sterile, solitary cubicle. The initial thrill of spending her days with small

children had worn off, and Donna felt a sharp loneliness whenever she had a moment to stop and reflect—which, granted, was
rare. Even when co-workers visited or passed her in the hall,
they addressed her as Ms. Moffett, and seemed to expect the
same formality from her. It was a public school ritual that
seemed strangely cold.

Even more, Donna caught herself feeling a nagging sense of
tedium as she sounded out the letter B, wrote "kite" and "cat" on
the chalkboard, or helped the students count plastic chips and
fake coins. A secretary's work may not be brain surgery, but
Donna found intellectual challenges in writing Gerry's letters—
there was always a new phrase or tone to try out—planning the
logistics of a company retreat, or resolving spats between co-
workers. Now she was sitting cross-legged on a grimy tiled floor,
banging a tambourine and leading rounds of "Good Ship Lollipop."

This was a higher calling? How long could she tolerate reciting
the alphabet five days a week, or the patience-trying repetition of
lining children up from tallest to shortest, sharpening their
stubby pencils and pulling them off the floor? She had hoped for
a third- or fourth-grade class, figuring that eight- or nine-year-
olds would have shed nursery habits, yet not present frightening
behavior problems or apathy. Indeed, her earliest sharp memory
of herself as a student was as a third-grader, on a class trip to the
Guggenheim Museum, where she had been transfixed by Van
Gogh's sunflowers. But third- and fourth-graders were largely
out of the question for novices like Donna. These were major
testing grades, the first in which children took the make-or-
break city and state exams in reading and math. P.S. 92, which
risked being closed if its test scores did not improve that year,
could not afford to put teaching fellows in those grades.

Diana Rahmaan had not wanted to hand over any classroom to a teaching fellow, actually. She had planned to make all three of her fellows "cluster teachers" who traveled from room to room, teaching science or social studies and doing as little damage as possible.

But when a veteran first-grade teacher took a job on Long Island at the last minute, Rahmaan gave her class to Donna, the oldest of her fellows by over a decade. It was hardly a casual decision because, unbeknownst to Donna, the class was a difficult one, full of children with behavior and learning problems. The risk was all the greater because, despite the tedium of the daily routine, first grade is a critical year.

Although many—probably even most—of New York's public school children do not learn to read by the end of first grade, their teacher has to start them on their way—an awesome responsibility, paradoxically defined by mundane tasks and routines. These children, still relatively unscarred by the long-term effects of poverty, ill-equipped parents, crime-ridden neighborhoods, and bad schools, can still be reached, according to the research. They are at the age when lifelong habits begin to form, a time of precedent-setting successes and confidence-building, or of failures and neglect. If a child is not reading by the fourth grade, the research goes, they will likely take several more years to learn, falling into the rut of being held back in their grade and losing interest in school. First grade, then, is crucial—some European and Asian countries allow only the most experienced instructors to preside over early-childhood classrooms.

In Flatbush, though, there are not nearly enough experienced teachers to staff any grade. Only 44 percent of P.S. 92's teachers had more than five years on the job when Donna arrived. So she found herself charged with a job that was equal parts awesome and mundane, feeling alternately like a savior and like a fraud.

.   .   .

Even lessons in courtesy, on which Donna prided herself the most, did not seem to be sinking in. From the beginning, courtesy had been a watchword in Room 218: Donna made the students say "please" and "thank you" and shake hands after a disagreement, a practice that seemed foreign to them. But too often, these lessons in character education came at the expense of reading, math, social studies, and science.

When Stefanie punched Briella in the stomach one day as the class was returning from lunch, Donna grabbed each girl by the shoulder and marched them to the front of the classroom to trade apologies in front of the other students. "Briella, I want you to tell Stefanie how you felt when she punched you," she said. Briella was still sobbing from the blow.

"I feel sad," Briella, chubby and adorable, wailed as her classmates watched with open mouths. The youngest of three sisters, Briella had perfected such a wounded, angelic look that most people found it hard to stay mad at her for long.

"And Stefanie, how do you feel when you see Briella cry?" Donna asked.

Stefanie hesitated, shifting her weight from one foot to the other, clearly unused to this form of punishment.

"I feel angry," Stefanie finally announced. When Donna asked her to elaborate, she stared at the back of the room for thirty seconds. Introspection was not her strong suit. Like Briella, she lacked control over her emotions and often put them ostentatiously on display. But while Briella acted out by crying,

Stefanie did so in violent bursts of energy: shrieking, running to the front of her classroom to wrap her strong little arms around Donna, or, as in this case, slugging a classmate.

"I feel angry because she hit me in the back," Stefanie said, adding a new wrinkle to the plot. Briella sobbed louder and Donna ordered her to stop. "Are you girls going to apologize to each other?"

After what seemed an eternity—Jamilla had begun teaching her seatmates a dance move and a few of the boys were peering at a toy catalog that one of them had smuggled in—Stefanie muttered, "Sorry."

"Sorry *what?*" Donna yelled. "What is her *name?*" She had told them time and again to look each other in the eye and address each other by name when apologizing. If she couldn't teach them this, her thinking went, she couldn't teach them anything.

Stefanie tried again: "I'm sorry, Briella. I'm sorry that I hurt you."

Under Donna's expectant glare, Briella replied, "Sorry Stefanie that I . . . hurt you." They shook hands, and Donna, satisfied, turned to the rest of the class.

"Boys and girls, there must be peace," she said. "No hurting."

.   .   .

The drama had taken twenty minutes of the math lesson and made the students restless and distracted. By 1:15, Jamal would not sit down, and Donna ended up chasing him into a corner and growling, "This is not a game of tag." So many students were talking out of turn that she started a list and announced that the talkers could not go to computer lab that afternoon. It proved an ineffective threat; by the time a seventh name landed on the list, she upped the ante, raising the possibility of canceling their participation in the Halloween parade the following week.

Christopher had been howling like a werewolf for nearly ten minutes but stopped when Donna marched toward his desk. "I don't hear you howling anymore," she said sharply. "Why aren't you howling?" Then, in a display of emotion as unrestrained as Stefanie's or Briella's, she leaned toward him and howled loudly: "Ah-*oooh*! Ah-*oooh*!"

For once, Donna had silenced the room. The class stared at her anxiously, not sure what to expect next. The mood in Room 218 was suddenly one of hopelessness, the children despondent and the teacher looking on the verge of tears. All the sunny posters and the books with blithe titles—*A Pocketful of Stars, Someone I Like*—were jarringly at odds with the prevailing gloom. Donna's shoulders slumped and she closed her eyes briefly as she turned away from Christopher and toward the front of the classroom. She was ashamed, and did not want to face her students for another minute that day.

Throughout the city, other teaching fellows were having their own versions of the howling incident—losing their self-control over disruptive behavior. In the Bronx, a former judge hit a middle school student on the head with an eraser when the boy would not stop mouthing off. The boy complained, and the teacher was removed from the classroom on disciplinary charges. A year later, another fellow in the Bronx would slam a paperweight on a girl's desk in an attempt to silence a noisy fifth-grade class and hit her finger, severing the tip. That fellow would be arrested and charged with third-degree assault.

When it finally came time for computer lab, Donna lined up all but the seven students whose misbehavior had lost them the privilege. Briella sobbed as Donna ordered her and the other six to lay their heads on their desks. The others waited in the hall for Paul Herbold, the computer teacher, to pick them up—but after three minutes he still had not arrived. Donna called the office and learned that Herbold was out sick. Her lingering shame was eclipsed by anger; how could no one have bothered to tell her? She listened to Briella sob and steeled herself to resist sobbing, too.

A more experienced teacher might have whipped out a math worksheet or conjured up a word game to fill the last forty minutes of the day. But Donna could not stand in front of her class for another minute; her patience was shot and she feared losing control and humiliating herself again. Besides, their coats were on, their backpacks slung around their small shoulders—because it was the last period of the day, they took all their belongings to computer lab on Fridays and Herbold dismissed them. Donna looked out the window for the first time that afternoon, saw brilliant October sunshine, and let impulse guide her once again. She was risking Robertson's wrath, but since nobody had bothered to tell her about Herbold's absence, she did not particularly care.

"Boys and girls, who would like to go to the playground?" she asked the lined-up students. Whoops and cheers ensued, and within five minutes the students were racing around a small, fenced-in playground that was normally reserved for kindergartners. As Donna basked in the sun and the crisp air, Curtis sidled up and described the Darth Vader costume he would wear on Halloween. Christopher, after whooshing down the slide a few times, happily told her that he would dress as a wrestler. Donna marveled at how a little fresh air and exercise calmed and cheered them. Was she a savior or a fraud? She would not let herself entertain that question for the rest of the day.

CHAPTER FOUR

By November, the Teaching Fellows program itself was flailing. About three dozen of the 323 fellows who had started teaching in September had quit, victims of culture clash, impossibly high expectations, unmanageable discipline problems, and crushing disillusionment. The media attention lavished on the program through the summer and early fall had waned, and just as many fellows were realizing their notions of teaching had been fantastical, many of their superiors were denouncing Harold Levy's early promises about the program as empty propaganda.

Many superintendents and principals resented how Levy had foisted it on them late in the summer, exhorting them to pay special attention to the fellows and do whatever it took to get them up to speed. Teachers felt increasingly bitter that these newcomers were getting public kudos and free master's degrees, when so many of them were still paying off their graduate school loans. The resentment ran deep; even Randi Weingarten, the president of the New York City teachers' union, who had publicly endorsed the program, had begun privately soothing traditionally trained teachers with statements like, "I don't blame you for hating them."

Levy was deeply conflicted: He wanted the fellows to feel like an elite corps, and to see him as their unflinching champion. But three months into his grand experiment, Levy had reluctantly decided to distance himself from the fellows and—publicly, at least—stop painting them as the school system's salvation.

It was a wrenching decision. He wanted this program to be his legacy to the school system. He still believed deeply in its potential. And he hated this notion, so deeply ingrained in the culture of public schools, that everyone should be treated just the same. How exasperating, for example, that teachers could be rated only 'S' (satisfactory) or 'U' (unsatisfactory), when there were so many nuances involved. Though he respected the teachers' union for so vigorously protecting its own interests, Levy also wanted to weaken its defense of the status quo, just as many of his predecessors had. Creating the Teaching Fellows program was a good start, he hoped: The fellows were a proactive bunch who he hoped would get involved with the union, urging it to be more progressive and challenging the old, inflexible ways that many veterans zealously guarded.

The United Federation of Teachers, like so many other teachers' unions, had organized in the 1960s with the noble intentions of protecting teachers from unfair treatment and elevating the profession's status. Because of the size of its membership and the remarkable savvy of one of its first leaders, the charismatic Albert Shanker, the union amassed power quickly. After the community-control battles of the late '60s, when a black administrator had summarily transferred white teachers and adminstrators out of the Ocean Hill–Brownsville district in Brooklyn, the wary union had pushed hard to end local flexibility in hiring and firing. In exchange for supporting the creation of local school boards in the early 1970s, the union won changes in state education law that made it nearly impossible to fire tenured teachers.

The union's political might grew with its active membership, which went from just 2,500 in 1960 to over 100,000 in 2000. Another strength was the longevity of union leaders: While governors, mayors, chancellors, and Board of Ed members turned over quite often, Al Shanker headed the United Federation of Teachers for twenty-two years, and his successor, Sandra Feldman, for another eleven. The union's institutional memory and political connections were second to none, and those with less tenure—chancellors and board members in particular—found themselves turning to it for advice on steering the ship.

If they resisted the union's proposals, or proposed something the union didn't like, it could appeal to Albany, which had considerable power over New York City education policy. The union, like others around the country, gave generously to political campaigns, and in return, expected lawmakers to back its priorities. If they didn't, the union could block their re-elections with well-organized drives and expensive advertising.

New York City was not especially generous with raises over the years—whereas its teachers were generally better paid than those in other cities, those with experience could make far more money just across the New Jersey, Connecticut, and Westchester County borders. Instead, in contract after contract, the city conceded on work rules, helping the union accumulate power through the '70s, '80s, and '90s.

Many of these one-size-fits-all rules governed teacher work schedules, so that a principal could not ask his staff to work extra hours or days, or even to monitor playgrounds, cafeterias, and hallways. All teachers were entitled to a fifty-minute, duty-free lunch break, and to at least one "prep period" during their six-hour, twenty-minute work day, during which their superiors could not assign them work. It was partly because of these rules that the teaching force had grown so large, for extra bodies were needed to cover classrooms while teachers took their preps.

More vexing were rules that hindered a school's ability to re-cruit the kind of teachers it needed most. One allowed senior teachers from anywhere in the system to transfer into a school to fill a job opening without so much as an interview. The union was also reluctant to allow higher starting salaries for teachers with expertise in shortage areas like science or math, or bonuses for those whose students' test scores improved, because it wanted all its members treated equally. It also insisted that sen-ior teachers choose their own assignments, so that principals often could not put their strongest teachers in the most chal-lenging classrooms. Though principals could technically veto a teacher's job choice, most did not out of fear that the teacher would file a time-consuming grievance.

Which is not to say the union *always* blocked out-of-the-box proposals. The Chancellor's District was an admirable example of how the union could be flexible, with limits: It had agreed to a longer teacher workday in exchange for 15 percent higher salaries in forty desperate schools, though it was picky about how the extra forty minutes per day could be used. In an earlier contract, the union had agreed to let schools opt out of many work-rule provisions in its contract—if most of their staff voted to do so. But since these occasional compromises affected only a limited number of schools, they did not lead to widespread change.

How frustrating, Levy thought, that the union contract forced him to send the fellows to the most daunting environ-ments from the get-go. Too bad they could not start out in calmer schools where they would face fewer demoralizing obstacles, then transfer to the failing schools once they had a year or two of experience. And how sad that petty resentments were plaguing this group who had answered his summons so eagerly, taking on the students that so many veteran teachers shunned.

But in distancing himself from the fellows and telling them to instead find support among their colleagues, Levy risked alienating them to the point when many might leave. Worse, he thought, they might lose the subversive, us-versus-them mentality that made them so potentially powerful in a system so afraid of risk and wedded to the status quo.

Vicki Bernstein, however, was convinced otherwise. She, more than Levy, had fielded the complaints from principals and superintendents about the fellows' performance, and from the fellows about their colleagues' hostility. In her mind a blatantly rebellious attitude was foolish, as there were only 300 fellows (because many had quit) in a system of 5,000 administrators and 80,000 teachers. Levy would not be the chancellor forever—he'd be lucky to hold onto the job for another year or two—and there was no guarantee his successors would champion or even keep the Teaching Fellows program. The best that he could do, Bernstein believed, was to minimize the potential for resentment and encourage the fellows to blend in. The good ones would know how valued they were without Levy's praise and quietly, humbly set an example for their more jaded colleagues. She entreated Levy to stop glorifying the program in speeches and interviews, and to let the fellows know that he could not afford them his constant protection.

"I didn't like it at all," Levy said later. "But I decided I had to do it. The system could not coddle them and by implication do less for the others. What I could do was give them as good a preparation as possible, then set them on a course so that in the fullness of time, they would change the way the system thought of itself."

·   ·   ·

By late November, Bernstein had persuaded Levy to hold a meeting with the fellows and signal his change of view. Donna Moffett hurried back to Manhattan that afternoon, hopeful that reconnecting with the chancellor and her fellow missionaries would give her the strength to make it through to Christmas.

The meeting took place at a high school in the affluent Gramercy Park neighborhood; Donna arrived late and stood in the back of the room, self-conscious. Most of the other fellows present were in their twenties and thirties and gave off an intensity that suggested they were not soft-around-the-edges idealists—not anymore, anyway.

Levy also arrived late, his burly bodyguard waving off the eager fellows who attempted to intercept him on his way to the lectern. Levy had shared his e-mail address with the fellows at the August convocation ceremony, in a show of accessibility. But to the fellows' annoyance, he had been passing most of their e-mails onto aides instead of answering them himself. Except for a few who had staked out his office or his public appearances, most had not heard from Levy since that emotional summer day at LaGuardia High.

They crowded close to the chancellor, who wore an arch, amused expression that seemed wrong for the occasion. There were no chairs, so everyone was standing with tensed shoulders, crossed arms, and, in a few cases, clenched fists. Levy held up his arms in a theatrical bid for silence, then gestured for everyone to step back. Before listening, he said, he wanted to be heard. He

said he felt their pain, but also pleaded for patience and asked
them to cut him some slack as he figured out how to make the
program work.

"The good news is you're through the worst of it," Levy said.
"The bad news is you've still got to get through the rest of it. I
don't doubt that's an uphill battle."

What an understatement.

"I'm impressed by the degree of criticism you're imposing on
yourselves," Levy continued. "I don't think you realize how *good*
you are."

Levy reminded the fellows that many of their principals were
novices, too. Of the system's 1,200 principals, three hundred had
fewer than two years on the job, he said, and "don't know how to
give positive reinforcement."

Levy said he had also heard that many assistant principals
were unhelpful and even hostile to the fellows, which comforted
Donna. Maybe she shouldn't take Robertson's wrath so personally, she thought.

Then Levy said something that made the crowd squirm. Instead of promising to lean on principals to support the program,
he urged the fellows to seek support from each other, from other
teachers, and from their union. He offered sympathy, but made
it clear he was not going to fight their battles.

"I don't have the slightest doubt that there are future principals in this room," Levy said. "It's the people with a different
cut, a different slice, who have the best potential to be good
teachers. If quality people are there, then we can do anything,
because then the system can move along.

"You are the cutting edge of where we need to make this system go," Levy went on, his voice rising. "What you need to do is
pull the rest of the system with you."

To an extent, this was just what the fellows wanted to hear, a repeat of what he had told them in August. But while that first rousing speech had given the fellows an impassioned sense of shared mission, this one left them wrestling with far more complicated emotions.

Here Levy was, admitting that many principals did not appreciate the fellows or even know how to run their schools. But Levy was the chancellor—the only one who could coax their superiors to treat them well, or change some of the maddening rules governing their classrooms. And yet instead of promising, "I'll make sure they learn to appreciate you," he was only saying, "Stick together and do the best you can." How could they be Levy's shock troops if he was unwilling to lead the charge?

Donna, for one, felt betrayed. Depend on one another? As if that would carry her through June? As if it would help her teach Curtis and Stefanie to read, and keep Christopher and Trevor from climbing the walls? The young crowd up front had already begun bombarding Levy with complaints, still hoping he could be persuaded to come to their rescue. Donna tensed with recognition and surprise as she heard them list everything she hated about her new job. One young man bitterly recounted the hours he spent "wallpapering" his classroom and the bulletin board outside it with writing and artwork that met a specific "learning objective." Teachers in failing schools were required to wallpaper so that inspectors would see evidence, however superficial, that the students were hard at work. Another fellow complained that the math curriculum in the Chancellor's District was "just entertainment." Another bemoaned the ridiculous lack of instructional time, between all the visitors churning through classrooms, fire drills, mundane public address announcements, and the shuffling of children to and from Success for All.

One man asked about rumors that several fellows had already gotten "unsatisfactory" ratings from their assistant principals. The crowd fell silent. Getting a "U" was almost unheard of—the teachers' union contract made it nearly impossible for principals to justify it, since they had to scrupulously document a teacher's poor performance and the teacher could file endless appeals.

Levy clucked, shook his head, and promised to check into the matter. He glanced pointedly at his watch, but the fellows were not ready to let him go. One woman announced that many of the students at her school had been physically and sexually abused, and that just this month, a father had raped his daughter. Another said that students had assaulted two teachers at her school in the last two weeks, and returned to school after brief suspensions.

"There are at least four kids in every class who are *absolutely* not fit for regular classrooms," the woman barked. Donna counted to herself: Luis, Jamal, Cindy, Christopher.

It was dark outside now; Levy was done. Almost as an afterthought, he said: "I'm going to tell the superintendents to get the message out to principals that this is a program they are to *embrace*." It was his only applause line. He felt guilty as he hustled out of the gymnasium, but grudgingly convinced that distancing from the fellows was the only way to ensure his program survived.

·   ·   ·

Donna walked into the frigid night with a woman she recognized from her summer training, who had worked on Wall Street. The woman was marveling at how little her fourth-graders knew of life outside East New York, a desolate Brooklyn neighborhood that made Flatbush look suburban. She talked about reading them *The Lion, the Witch and the Wardrobe,* the first book in the C. S. Lewis series about the enchanted land of Narnia, and about how she had brought in Turkish delight for them to taste. The sticky candy was a heavenly treat for one of the young characters, but the woman said she had been amazed to find that none of her students had heard of Turkish delight, much less tasted it.

Donna thought of her own battles against the blue juice and chips doused in fake orange cheese; at first she had scolded her students about bringing in such unhealthy snacks, even threatening to take them away on a few occasions and give them apples instead. But then Donna had realized it was not only useless, but patronizing to object to foods that her students' parents had given them. Had the East New York students liked the Turkish delight, she asked?

No, the woman said; they'd spit it out.

. . .

On the cold, bright Thursday before Thanksgiving, Donna emerged from the subway just four minutes before eight, an early bird no more. She hurried past the dingy warehouses lining the long block toward P.S. 92, cringing as a sharp wind stung her face.

"These children are going to take everything I have," she murmured. She looked toward the massive school building, and to her horror, she started to cry.

Donna had held her first conferences with parents the night before, and, in her mind, things had not gone well. Four children's parents, including Stefanie's mother, never showed, even though Donna had sent home several reminders. Trevor's step-father had demanded to know why the boy could not write a sentence, and Donna could only stare at him mutely.

Irwin Kurz from the Chancellor's District had been sending an "instructional specialist" into Donna's classroom to observe and give advice, a favor he hoped would bolster Donna's spirit and confidence. The specialist, Dakota Reyes, was glamorous for a Board of Ed bureaucrat, with rows of long braids, elaborate makeup, and pungent perfume. She worked for Kurz in the district office but spent much of her time in troubled schools, trying to help overwhelmed or under-qualified teachers master the Chancellor's District routines. Kurz had asked her to check up on Donna after his brief visit to Room 218 before Halloween, when he had decided Donna had a particularly challenging class.

But over the course of several mornings, Reyes had barely witnessed any instruction. Instead, she had seen Trevor hoot incessantly, Cindy throw a tantrum, and Curtis drop to the floor cackling. She had also seen Donna lose her cool, stomping and shouting.

Meanwhile, Donna had missed her graduate course at Brooklyn College three weeks in a row. The course, "Learning to Teach Math," was to provide three of the thirty credits she needed for permanent certification. The Board of Ed had the teaching fellows taking one evening graduate class a week, but even that felt overwhelming to many of them during this first semester. The schedule was especially hard on perfectionists like Donna, who desperately wanted to keep control over their lives and be topflight teachers and students at once.

Donna found so much to do in her classroom after school that she almost never made it to Brooklyn College, four subway stops away in Flatbush, by 6:00 p.m. As the streetlamps came on and other teachers clicked their doors shut for the night, she would grade and hang her students' work; go over the next day's Success for All script; clean up the daily mess of paper scraps, pencil stubs, chalk, and snack wrappers; and straighten the well-trafficked story corner. Sometimes she would rearrange the little desks, hoping that a new configuration would make one child more attentive, another less likely to pester a neighbor. Those silent hours alone in her classroom soothed and sustained Donna, perhaps because they were the only time she had everything under control. She was embarrassed of her truancy, but "Learning to Teach Math" was deathly dull and, in fact, had little relevance to her daily routine.

Donna, a maestro of scheduling at Flemming, Zulack, couldn't even plan her own weekends now. On Saturday she was supposed to attend a seminar for the teaching fellows, organized by the superintendent of the Chancellor's District and led by principals who were going to talk about the curriculum. But Saturday was also the day of a family birthday party in New Jersey, and Donna's relatives were badgering her to attend. They had never had to badger before, but now Donna's schedule overwhelmed her, and choices were never clear-cut.

.   .   .

For weeks, Donna had felt as if she were trapped in a centrifuge—as if she were being whipped into tiny particles and re-constituted into something unrecognizable. In bed at night, her mind raced from one problem to another, then fell into anxious dreams that often woke her. In one, she had lost her glasses and was groping blindly. In another, she was picking through trash, frantic to find something she had lost. She felt scorned, distrusted, derelict, exhausted, and deeply ashamed. She was failing a roomful of children and their parents—not beginning to live up to the teaching fellows' goal of helping all the city's children get a sound education.

Donna had taken on that noble, impossible mission with heartbreaking seriousness. The Board of Education had marketed it so effectively with "Sad Girl," as board officials called the poignant newspaper ad that had drawn thousands. Recruits like Donna—altruistic types with vague longings to do good and little experience with poverty, other races, or even public-school culture—were floundering as their simplistic perceptions of teaching ran up hard against reality.

The best principals and other administrators could harness the energy and enthusiasm of people like Donna, using it constructively—with plenty of friendly supervision—instead of rolling their eyes at it. But Donna had barely spoken to Diana Rahmaan since September, other than exchanging pleasantries in the main office.

To make matters worse, Donna could feel herself hardening against some of her charges as they sapped every ounce of her energy and brainpower. She was haunted by the memory of howling at Christopher that day before Halloween, setting a terrible example for the class. And yet she could muster barely any warmth toward Christopher. She knew she could be a good teacher if children like him wouldn't wreak havoc on her classroom and her sanity. Her expectations for the students were as high as for herself, and the disappointment when they let her down was crushing.

She stopped at the corner bodega, allowing self-pity to engulf her for half a minute before she blotted at her tears with the sleeve of her puffy down parka and walked the remaining half-block to the school steps.

Then she pulled open the door to P.S. 92, drew a long, forti-fying breath, and went in.

The warmth and bustle of the place enveloped her as she walked the few steps to the main office. She punched the time clock and waved to Vera Pavone, her favorite school secretary, who waved back with her usual wry smile. She passed Jim Raf-fel, her Teaching Fellow friend who taught on the fourth floor, in the hall and he patted her arm in solidarity. Jim, too, was struggling to survive at P.S. 92: His fourth- and fifth-grade stu-dents, much bigger and tougher than Donna's little ones, got into regular fistfights, and one girl whose fight he had broken up had accused him of hitting her.

Upstairs, late autumn sunlight flooded Room 218 as the ten students who had arrived on time noisily took off their coats and peppered her with breathless news bulletins: Ms. Moffett, I got Doritos for lunch! Ms. Moffett, it's my sister's birthday! Look, Ms. Muffin, I tied my own shoes!

There was no time for self-reflection when she was among them, and today, it was just as well. As she bent down to look and listen, putting an arm around one child and fixing another's collar, she had no choice but to soldier on. The weight of her sadness eased, for now.

.   .   .

Donna's class roster had shrunk from twenty to seventeen. A boy named Michael, who had left in early October for what was supposed to be a two-week visit with family in Jamaica, had not returned. The word from the office was that Michael's mother had put him in school in Kingston, thinking he would have a better chance of a good education there.

Luis had been transferred to another school at the beginning of October, as Brenda Robertson had foretold. And just last week, Jamal, an out-of-control boy Donna could do nothing with, was sent back to kindergarten. Donna had asked few questions; she had the other students and herself to look out for.

One other problem child, a volatile Haitian-American boy named Julian, might also be leaving: His mother had said during her conference with Donna that they might move to Montreal after Christmas. Donna hoped it would happen, because Julian had been having temper tantrums to rival Cindy's. He had spun into a rage when Donna tried to send him to the back of the room one day, and his fury had shocked her. The boy had shoved a chair into Shakeela, making her cry, and kicked other students' chairs as if possessed. He had told Donna that he missed his father, who was living in Florida.

As a jazzy tune came over the public address system at 8:45, signaling the start of Success for All, Dakota Reyes, the instructional specialist sent by the Chancellor's District, strode in with a lipstick smile. She quietly took a seat in the back as Donna chided three girls who were dancing to the Success for All song and getting stirred up. Reyes was sympathetic to Donna and wanted to help, but Donna was unnerved by her visits, during which she sat silently in the back of the room and took notes, then pointed out things she thought Donna could be doing better.

"If we are fooling around, maybe people will think we're foolish," Donna said, aware that Reyes was watching for signs that she could not control the class. "But if we act smart, then maybe people will see how smart we really are."

The Success for All story today was "The Class Trip," about first-graders from the city who visit a farm. The sunshine and the children's affection had cheered and energized Donna, and her presentation of the lesson showed she had made some progress with the reading program since October. Sticking to the drill, she had the class make predictions based on the pictures in their books.

"Do you know what kind of water the duck is swimming in, Patrick?" she asked. Patrick squinted at a drawing of a ball flying toward a pond, and replied: "Dirty water." Donna laughed.

Trevor's prediction was so good that she wrote it on the board: "The ball falls in the water. The duck feels mad." Although Trevor was still misbehaving a lot and lapsing into baby talk, he was showing more interest in learning, perhaps because Donna was making it more enjoyable than what Trevor had experienced in kindergarten. He would hunch over his notebook and stare at the blackboard with an intensity that surprised Donna. When she wasn't looking, he would stuff books from the reading corner into his backpack.

Donna threw her body into the lesson, bowing low and slowly straightening back up as she made the sound of M: mmmm-mmm. The students loved it, laughing appreciatively and wiggling their own torsos. They loved it, too, when she veered from the script to remind them of the field trip they had taken earlier that week, to a farmers' market in Brooklyn Heights. But Reyes, jotting in a notebook, looked pained. In her mind, playfulness was out of the question with students this restless and a reading program this rigid. Donna was just stirring these children up and making their attention spans even shorter.

"Should Ms. Moffett go home?" Donna asked playfully, trying a little humor to get the class to quiet down. After feeling such despair that morning, she was fishing for a reminder of how much they needed her. "Should I just go on home?"

"Nooooo!" the kids shouted. Stefanie jumped up to grab her teacher around the legs and make sure she stayed right there. Dakota Reyes made a note to herself to get Donna more help— at the very least, a more experienced colleague to "model" Success for All for her, to impress on her the benefits of sticking to the script. Reyes had never seen so many children in one class who could not keep still; even a veteran teacher would have a hard time keeping order and conducting smooth lessons, she thought.

Donna took the class to the back of the room to read *Whistle for Willie* by Ezra Jack Keats. But by page 3, Trevor had grabbed the book from her hands, and she tried her misguided trick of making him "our new teacher." Christopher delivered the book back to Donna, but then promptly began hopping around the circle, as if playing Duck, Duck, Goose. Curtis said, "They have too many black people in this book," prompting a withering look from Donna and a flurry of new notes in Reyes's book. The lesson stopped and started, started and stopped like a sputtering engine.

Nicole Peat sat quietly at Donna's elbow, brow furrowed, eyes on the book, face strained. With excruciating patience, she was waiting to learn.

.   .   .

By the time the students returned from lunch, Dakota Reyes was gone and Donna had lost the adrenaline that had propelled her through the morning. She was feeling near tears again. Instead of doing math, she told the children to write about whatever they wanted while she comforted herself by tidying the room. As usual, the students were all over the place: Shakeela, who had read *Jamberry* so skillfully in September, quickly whipped off a sloppy but perfectly spelled story about visiting the beach. Nicole wanted to write about a cat, but had to ask Shakeela how to spell every word. Jamilla, who was close to reading but whose adolescent-like moodiness was a handicap, took a book from the reading corner and copied random lines from it. Two boys drew action heroes and sneaked looks at a toy catalogue one of them had smuggled in.

After school, Donna squeezed into the chair usually occupied by Cindy and laid her head on the smudged, sticky desk. Her eyes were downcast and dull. "I am a complete failure," she murmured.

.   .   .

In Donna's classroom, the conveyor belt of visitors chugged on, an example of Board of Ed protocol that looked promising on paper but was more often an unorganized waste of money and time. The morning after Dakota Reyes's visit, Room 218 had another guest, Nina Wasserman, an education professor whom Brooklyn College had assigned to observe Donna periodically and give her advice. This was another perk of the Teaching Fellows program, which the schools had no choice but to tolerate. Like Reyes, Wasserman exuded a calm sophistication that made her stand out among the hurly-burly of P.S. 92. The students seemed awed by both women, staring at them and politely following their directions. Though Brenda Robertson's visits had a similar effect, she usually appeared harried and could not afford to stay long. Reyes and Wasserman came for at least an hour and struck the children as dignitaries from another, more formal world.

But Reyes's and Wasserman's missions could not have been more different. As a standard-bearer for the Chancellor's District, Reyes defended regimented programs like Success for All as the last, best chance for helping vulnerable children—especially since so many of their teachers were inexperienced or otherwise weak. She thought that students in failing schools needed the discipline and strict routine they would never get outside school.

Wasserman, on the other hand, fell into the progressive camp of educators. Her general philosophy was that children had different strengths and weaknesses, and that teachers should tailor the approach to fit the child. A one-size-fits-all model like Success for All ran counter to her idea of good teaching, since it demanded every child to learn the same thing every day, in the exact same amount of time.

But Wasserman had never encountered a school like P.S. 92 before she was put in charge of Donna; she and Donna were equally perplexed by the ways of the Chancellor's District. Most of Wasserman's Brooklyn College students did their student-teaching at schools that embraced the progressive approach, with middle-class students whose parents wanted a creative academic program with lots of hands-on projects. Most of these parents read to their children and provided other intellectual stimulation at home; they were not nearly as likely as Donna's students to struggle with the fundamentals of reading and writing.

Of the two women, Donna related more to Wasserman, with whom she had immediately clicked when they met in late October. They had similar interests: classical music, Broadway plays, gardening, museums. They swapped book recommendations and quirky stories they had heard on National Public Radio. Nina, who was in her early sixties and insisted that Donna call her by her first name—a rarity in a school system where teachers were on a last-name basis, as in the military—had quickly assumed a mothering role in Donna's life. She nudged her to leave Room 218 promptly after school, eat more balanced meals, get more sleep, and find more ways to relax on weekends. Donna was touched, since the other authority figures in her new life usually focused on how she was falling short and all that she needed to do better.

In the month that she had known Nina, Donna had spoken to her once or twice a week by phone, even calling on a few Saturdays to vent and be consoled. But while Nina would have liked to observe Donna more than once a month, her schedule could not accommodate more frequent visits.

When Nina came to Room 218 on the Friday before Thanksgiving, Donna happily sat down for a few minutes and let Nina show her what to do. It was different from other visits, when Donna felt like she was being judged and could not let down her guard for a second. Nina would never, for example, criticize Donna in front of her students, something others had done. She affirmed, even encouraged, Donna's disdain of the Chancellor's District curriculum and urged Donna to be true to herself as a teacher. In the "us-versus-them" scenario that Harold Levy had envisioned for his teaching fellows, Nina was firmly in the "us" category. And lonely Donna loved her for it.

Nina had arrived after lunch, for the afternoon literacy lesson. She had read a fanciful story about dogs, then led a spirited discussion about pets. When the students grew distracted, Nina had wisely passed out paper and crayons and instructed them to draw dogs for the ten minutes that remained of the lesson. They were still immersed in the task when the bell rang and Nina prepared to depart for Jim Raffel's classroom.

Donna, who had been observing from the back of the room, snapped out of her laid-back state. It was time for math, still her weakest subject by far. The children were equally unenthusiastic; many were still coloring poodles and dachshunds despite her instructions to take out their math workbooks. Given the constant monitoring of Donna's progress teaching literacy, the absence of supervision in math was astounding.

"We're done with dogs," she announced a bit sharply, picking up a piece of chalk and turning to the blackboard. "Everyone write the numeral zero."

As Donna wrote neat row of 0s, 1s, and 2s on the board, Cindy wandered over to her desk and rifled through papers. Christopher bounced up like a jack-in-the-box and began pushing his chair across the room. After the previous day's disaster with manipulatives, and a scolding from Dakota Reyes, the brightly colored pieces of plastic and wood remained in their box today. Students would pay more attention with no colorful objects to distract them, Reyes had said. Yet nobody except diligent Nicole was copying the numbers off the board. Who could blame them? Donna thought crossly, disdaining what she considered a tedious math lesson.

Trying to rouse their interest, she drew both a straight-bottomed 2 and a curly-bottomed 2, saying they could copy whichever they liked better. "Let me see you write a whole line of them," she pleaded with false cheer. By now, Christopher had discovered the box of manipulatives in the back of the room and grabbed a handful, bonking another boy over the head with them. Donna wheeled around, her face fierce.

"You may now leave the room," she growled.

"I don't wanna leave the room," Christopher whimpered, dropping to his knees.

"Baby!" scoffed Jamilla, the tall girl, leading others to follow suit.

Donna probably would have done well to ignore Christopher, who might have returned to his seat when he realized his stunt would not get her attention. But she still had a knee-jerk impulse to nip misbehavior in the bud, which she had learned from her summer training and was applying across the board instead of choosing her battles, as more experienced teachers did. Donna again asked Christopher to get up off the ground, but he refused to uncrumple, and his body was a dead weight. She gave up and returned to the blackboard, but the boy's crying nagged at her. Given no other solution, she beckoned Ruth Baptiste to take him to the principal's office.

The class was surprisingly quiet afterward. They spent the remaining ten minutes of math class counting different objects in the room: girls, boys, teachers, windows. When Cindy correctly counted the number of girls—an astonishing feat for her—Donna felt triumphant and rushed over to shake the girl's hand. The rest of the class, eager to share in their teacher's temporary joy, all stuck out their hands for her to shake. She circled the room and pumped them ceremoniously.

Christopher sat solitary in the main office, ignored by the adults who swirled in and out. Donna had erased him from her mind.

·   ·   ·

Later, Donna gave a spelling test on the simplest Success for All vocabulary words: *the, of, and, to, in.* But Cindy, unwilling or perhaps unable to repeat her earlier success, left her paper blank. Manette and Stefanie asked Jamilla how to spell *in*, prompting Donna to thunder, "THERE IS NO TALKING DURING THE TEST!" When she caught Stefanie eyeing Jamilla's answers three minutes later, Donna ripped her paper into tiny pieces and took her pencil away. "I'm *very* disappointed, Stefanie," she said. "You may put your head down now."

Things had been steadily deteriorating since Nina left. Impulsively, Donna decided to skip that day's social studies lesson and hold a "class council"—a speak-out of sorts, for every student to discuss whatever was bothering him or her. Class councils were part of the Success for All curriculum—teachers were encouraged to hold them once a week to "identify positive classroom behaviors and solve classroom problems," according to the Success for All Foundation's Web site.

Donna had held a few class councils after what she considered moral breakdowns in Room 218: Jamilla's bossy bullying, for example, or Cindy's stealing. They were a good chance to gauge whatever problems or complicated feelings her students were struggling with in any given week.

Stefanie went first, announcing that she wanted to go back to kindergarten. Nicole, whose model behavior was fast making her the teacher's pet, said she was happy because she liked school and liked to learn. Shane, on the other hand, was angry because Ms. Moffett had not let him go to the bathroom earlier. Briella was mad because she had a cut on her finger. Curtis was happy, but Donna's effusive response made him change his mind and say he was mad. He was such a mystifying puzzle; Donna had met his mother, a talkative, tough-acting young woman named Liana who was raising Curtis and his sister, a kindergartner, on her own, a few times now, but there was nothing obvious about her that would explain the boy's oddities.

"How many feelings do you have right now?" she asked Curtis. "A hundred and ninety-two," he grumbled, and she nodded. Only now, in her third month of teaching, could Donna believe it possible to experience so many feelings in one day.

.　　.　　.

Nina returned at 2:20 to watch Donna dismiss the class—"You needn't be so militant," she said of the line-up routine—and give her a pep talk. She adored Donna, and thought she brought enormous creativity and feeling to her classroom. But Nina also thought Donna's perfectionist tendencies put her in danger of burning out fast. She had never seen a new teacher so badly neglect her most basic needs, like eating three meals a day; nor had she ever seen a new teacher as sick as Donna was in October. Despite her lack of experience with schools like P.S. 92, Nina could and did provide the nurturing that Donna craved.

Donna brought out a Tupperware container of pita triangles, hummus, and carrot sticks—her new attempt at eating a healthful, if still belated, lunch—and slumped over one of the little desks. "This woman Dakota Reyes thinks I get too excited with the children," she told Nina glumly.

"But you're nurturing their ability to enjoy their world!" Nina said. "It's a purposeful enthusiasm. Your Success for All materials are constraining, but you breathe life into those materials. You make the best use of what you have."

Pride rushed through Donna, just as it had when Cindy correctly counted the number of girls in the room a few hours earlier. But then her eyes leaked tears of exhaustion and self-pity. Nina handed Donna a tissue from her purse and patted her back.

"I just want you to preserve your health and your spirit and your abilities," Nina said as Donna blotted her eyes. "You have so much inside you to begin with. You just need a great deal of support."

Donna pointed out a new mat in the reading corner made of brightly colored, interlocking foam pieces. A friend had ordered the mat for her, and it was the latest thing to get her in trouble. She had decided to assemble it that morning as a Friday treat, at the beginning of Success for All. But putting together the mat had so excited the students that they kept playing with it through the lesson, pulling it apart instead of listening to Donna. Dakota Reyes had just shaken her head.

"I couldn't let another day go by without sharing it with the children," Donna told Nina.

"Your exuberance got the better of you," Nina said, smiling. "It's a very difficult balance that you have to achieve. It takes a long time to develop the kind of balance that lets you use your exuberance and enthusiasm, yet still move the class along."

But how to be patient, Donna asked, when so many people were pressuring her to get these children reading and adding and subtracting and writing by June?

It was a matter, Nina said, of vanquishing her need to feel loved and approved of by everyone—especially people like Brenda Robertson, who seemed determined not to give her that satisfaction.

"You know what they say about Bill Clinton—that when he walks into a room of one hundred people and ninety-nine are happy to see him, his only reaction is to worry about the other one?" Nina said. "Well, my dear, that's you."

After extracting promises from Donna to take hot baths at night and get a subscription to the New York Philharmonic—something Donna had done each winter until now—Nina embraced her and left. It was almost 4:00, the sun was low, and Donna had promised she would not linger as she usually did.

She completed the first part of her routine, plucking litter off the floor, but then stopped and retrieved her black parka from its closet by the door. She crammed three stacks of papers into her tote bag, along with five student notebooks, her lesson planner, and two teacher guides. The box of manipulatives that Christopher had delved into was still askew. The learning centers needed straightening, and it was time to start planning her December bulletin board. But for perhaps the first time since September, Donna didn't care. She felt only flat relief as she walked down Parkside Avenue, noticing neither the street noise nor the stinging, strengthening wind.

.   .   .

The experiences of that week proved pivotal for Donna; whether out of exhaustion, depression, or sheer pragmatism, she began approaching her job more stoically. On one level it was encouraging, because she was more capable of keeping things moving and under control without trying so hard to bring her personality into everything she did. But it was also sobering, because for the first time, Donna was accepting the party line and knuckling under to a routine that instinct told her would not help the children or her in the long term.

As the Christmas break approached, she performed Success for All lessons as rhythmically as a metronome. She had given herself over to the staccato routine, and briskly called out instructions to the nine students in her SFA group a few days before Christmas. "Point to the next sentence. Point to the first word. *Tanya. Tugs. A. Backpack. On. The. Bus.* Point to the next sentence. *The. Backpack. Unsnaps.* Point to the next sentence. *Books. And. A. Ball. Pop. Out.*"

So the lesson went, dry and uninspired. When someone talked or looked up from her or his reader, Donna used a tactic she had discovered a few weeks earlier: snapping her fingers and pointing at the miscreant with a menacing look while continuing the lesson. It worked much more effectively than stopping to chastise and punish, or making the student the teacher, since it provided no diversion for the rest of the class. Dakota Reyes, who had dropped in to check Donna's progress, was beaming. "This is improvement!" she told Donna, and she was not wrong.

Most of the children were following mechanically, but Melissa Gordon was slouching lower and lower in her seat, head propped on her hand. Melissa, plump and soft-featured with pigtails that stood straight out, was a quiet student; Donna had not gotten to know her well.

Melissa had been a good student during the first month of school, but lately she had been pulling stunts like this—ignoring Donna's instructions and spacing out during lessons. Donna suddenly loomed over her desk, unsmiling. "You need to sit up straight and track the words," she told Melissa. "I want to see your finger on the word *books.*"

Donna knew that Melissa had a month-old brother; maybe the newborn's arrival was distracting her and making her sad. She felt sorry for Melissa, who had been increasingly sullen and withdrawn. But she was also irritated. If Donna was putting her all into teaching, why couldn't these children—especially the ones who seemed adequately socialized, like Melissa—respond in kind?

"Melissa, I need to see you read," she said, kneeling next to the girl's desk, taking her index finger and leading it across the page. "*I. Can. Get. The. Bug. With. The. Stick.*" But Melissa's finger was a dead weight. Her face grew blanker and she stayed silent. Donna whispered "I'm disappointed," then returned to the front of the room.

Soon Melissa's cheek was resting on her desk, her hand absently playing with a piece of paper. Donna, who had planned to ignore her, grew impatient.

"Melissa, should I call your mother right now?" she said, prompting the other students to stare at their wayward classmate. "I love the way Tasha and Nicole and Christopher are following instructions. Your classmates are doing so well."

Donna read a few more sentences of the story, then stopped to ask the prescribed questions about the text. "Melissa, what happened to Derek?" Melissa kicked her legs so nervously that she hit Tasha, her neighbor, who shouted, "Don't be doing that!" Donna was now furious.

"You can kick but you can't speak?" she said, bringing her face down to Melissa's. "What's the matter with you?"

The week before, Donna had had a similar experience with Jamilla, who was as defiant as Melissa but in a more puckish way. Melissa's misbehavior bespoke a lack of motivation; Jamilla's was about wanting to do her own thing, which Donna found more sympathetic.

In that earlier incident, Donna had sent a few students to the back of the room for a brief "writers' workshop." Jamilla was among them, and was composing a poem when Donna asked the group to rejoin the rest of the class. Jamilla had lingered after the others complied, her face contorting into a bigger frown every time Donna asked her to come to the reading corner. Ultimately, Donna dragged Jamilla to the perimeter and forced her into a chair, where she sat glowering through the story.

Marie Buchanan, the P.S. 92 teacher whom Diana Rahmaan had assigned to be Donna's mentor, would later say that Donna should have let Jamilla write. Buchanan was a black woman about Donna's age who had worked at P.S. 92 for fourteen years, mostly as a second-grade teacher. But under the principal who had preceded Rahmaan, Buchanan had been promoted to "early-childhood literacy specialist," and her main job was to make sure classroom teachers were following the prescribed reading curriculum. Jobs like hers were coveted: Since specialists did not have their own classrooms, their stress levels were much lower than teachers', yet their pay was higher.

Buchanan had begun visiting Donna's classroom more frequently as Robertson, busy with the supervision of all kindergarten and first-grade classrooms, became a rarer presence. Buchanan liked to give advice, and in this case, she would tell Donna that when children were reluctant to abandon a project, it sometimes made sense to let them continue.

This confused and frustrated Donna. She would not have been surprised to hear it from Nina, but her colleagues at P.S. 92 and even her summer instructors had told her never to let even one child ignore directions. Best to stop a lesson in its tracks until every student was behaving perfectly, they had said. How could she let Jamilla ignore the strict schedule and continue her activity of choice when the rest of the class had to follow directions?

The new, hard-nosed Donna discarded Buchanan's advice, which felt only like another attempt to remind her she could do no right. Why brook rebellions like Jamilla's and Melissa's? Donna had been urged to adopt a drill sergeant's mentality. Now she had done so.

CHAPTER FIVE

Donna worked herself especially hard the week before Christmas, throwing a party for the students and preparing a bag of dollar-store treats for each of them. She also brought gifts for Diana Rahmaan, Brenda Robertson, and the secretaries, wrapping them during the children's lunch hour and rushing them to the main office. The students, in turn, brought gifts for Donna, and watched ecstatically as she opened them and ooohed her delight: "volcanic" bubble bath from Briella, a squirrel-shaped music box from Julian, and from Jamilla, a scarf printed with praying hands.

Donna had always been gung-ho about Christmas, but this year, she figured that getting to her sister's house in the suburbs for Christmas dinner would be the most she could manage. Decorating a tree, unearthing her holiday records to play, and going all-out on presents—traditions Donna cherished—would require more energy than she possessed. She even decided to skip the holiday party at Flemming, Zulack the evening before the break began, staying late in her classroom to organize things instead.

The two-week break was an odd betwixt-and-between time for Donna, who felt disconnected from her old life and inclined to avoid the people, places, and habits that had defined it, yet not quite adjusted to her new world. She spent most of the gray, frigid days off puttering around her apartment, renewing her addiction to NPR and worrying about the coming months in Room 218. While others enjoyed the dash and dazzle of Christmas in New York, Donna declined several social invitations and instead sorted through mountains of worksheets, drawings, notebooks, and other materials that had accumulated in every corner of her home since August. While appalled by the disorder of her household, Donna also found she enjoyed sorting through the detritus of her life in 218 and thinking about the challenges to come. She felt nervous but refreshed when it was time to go back—that she returned at all was, in fact, a triumph. A dozen other teaching fellows had quit over the break, deciding they could not handle another six months like the four they had just endured.

Although Donna was looking forward to seeing the students again, she also braced herself for disappointments, predicting that things might be crazy in Room 218 after the long hiatus. She assumed that some students would have forgotten chunks of what they had learned since September—including the rules she had worked so hard to drill into them. She figured they would have received loads of presents and sugary treats, and that they might be distracted and hyper. So when she reported back to school on January 2, Donna resolved not to let her joy at seeing them temper the stern façade she had forced herself to assume.

But the children surprised her. Instead of acting out of control, most were oddly quiet, as if they had spent the break in a sedentary state that she needed to coax them out of. Stefanie, as usual, said "hungry" when Donna asked how she felt on the first morning back. When Donna asked if she had eaten breakfast during the vacation, Stefanie stared at the floor and said, "Uh-uh." After lunch that day, the normally rambunctious Christopher fell asleep at his desk, in the middle of the math lesson. "I stayed up late every night," he explained. Little Nicole seemed especially subdued. When Donna asked what she had done during Christmas break, the girl shrugged and answered, "Nothing." She did not raise her hand once during the first week back.

Nicole and her brother and father lived with relatives a few blocks from the school. Donna knew that they had moved to New York from Jamaica two summers earlier, and that Nicole's mother had stayed behind, though she didn't know why. The father, who seemed as sweet as Nicole but extremely shy in Donna's voluble presence, came to walk his children home most afternoons. He worked the graveyard shift at Rite Aid. Maybe Nicole had longed to return to Room 218 because it offered soothing consistency, only to find the constellation of students had changed in a way that threatened her own position.

During the first week back, new students drifted into Donna's classroom like snowflakes. There were three in all, arriving with little warning and only the vaguest hints about their backgrounds. First came Manuel Portillo, a pudgy boy whose brow seemed permanently furrowed with concern. Donna had heard that Manuel, his identical twin brother, and their mother had fled their apartment in the Bronx over the holidays because of domestic violence. For now, they were living in a safe house a few blocks from P.S. 92, and Manuel seemed intent on making his circumstances sound enviable. "We have one room all full of books, and comfortable beds," he told some of his new classmates, his dark eyes wide and grave.

Monique LeJean, whose mother spoke only Haitian-Creole, had arrived next, transferring from another Brooklyn school. Then came Angelique Springer, from Trinidad, with a mother who was strikingly pretty and well spoken. All three newcomers wore starchy new uniforms and followed Donna's every instruction, eager to please. To her delight, all three seemed bright and highly motivated. Manuel and Angelique could read well, and Monique was not far behind.

Manuel loved to raise his hand and answer questions—always correctly—and Angelique wrote full paragraphs that were a little more complex than what most of Donna's students produced. In one of her first essays, recounting what she had done at lunch one day, Angelique astounded Donna by writing six perfectly spelled sentences: "I eat my lunch. I ate chicken nuggets. I ate PBJ sandwiches. I did my work. I did not fight. Some students threw food."

Angelique could read all of the books that lined the story corner, spelled and wrote beautifully, and even seemed a whiz at math. Donna had observed that many of the children who came to P.S. 92 directly from Trinidad and Jamaica did well. The schools were strict down there, she had heard, and many, though not all, of the parents made sure that their children stayed disciplined about schoolwork once they got to Brooklyn.

Donna had seated Angelique next to Nicole, whom she figured would help Angelique feel right at home. But by the third day back, she was regretting her decision. Nicole was clearly uncomfortable in Angelique's presence, glancing at the girl's notebooks worriedly and erasing her own work until the pages tore. Angelique was just as tiny and cute as Nicole, but better dressed and seemingly better cared for. She was just as diligent a student, but with more innate ability. Now, when her spelling tests came back scarred with red marks, Nicole shook her head and looked ashamed. It would be natural for Nicole, who reveled in the attention Donna lavished on her, to fear Angelique might steal some of it away.

But if the new composition of the class vexed Nicole, it was a blessing for Donna. Julian had moved to Canada over the break, as his mother had hinted would happen. With Julian, Jamal, and Luis gone, and three well-behaved, academically promising students in their place, the dynamic in Room 218 already seemed calmer and the class more manageable. Donna's autumn would surely have been easier with this small difference in her class roster. For the first time, she wondered if the problems of those first few months were not so much a reflection of her own abilities as of the hand she had been dealt. Remembering Dakota Reyes's assessment of her class in November—"I've never seen so many children who just can't sit still"—Donna thanked fate for the small miracle of Angelique, Manuel, and Monique sitting quietly at their desks, paying attention and, she hoped, setting an example.

Tasha, like Julian, had not returned after the break. Just before Christmas, the girl's mother had told Donna that she was being evicted from her apartment on Flatbush Avenue, and that she was worried about finding a new home that she could afford. Donna now feared that Tasha and her mother had been driven from the neighborhood, possibly into homelessness. But when Brenda Robertson called Tasha's grandmother at the end of the first week, she learned that they were temporarily staying with relatives in Queens and would return.

The following Monday, a week before Martin Luther King, Jr.'s birthday, Tasha reappeared in a chic, tight new outfit that Donna thought more suitable for a teenager than a six-year-old. Though her mother could not pay her rent, she always dressed her daughter in flashy, expensive-looking clothes. On this morning, Tasha's toy cell phone was clipped to her belt, and Donna kept catching her holding imaginary conversations to entertain her seatmates. After two warnings failed, Donna put the phone in the plastic, bear-shaped jug that had held animal crackers the first week of school. Now, it was brimming with contraband toys and candy that she had snatched from children who made the mistake of showing them off during class.

.   .   .

P.S. 92, like schools around the country, encouraged its teachers to incorporate the life and teachings of Dr. King into their January lesson plans. Donna saw the holiday as a chance to experiment with so-called character education—a subject she felt better equipped to teach than math, social studies, even reading. The concept of character education had gained national popularity after the school shootings in Columbine in 1999 and others that followed. President Bush had called for mandatory character education on the campaign trail, and now, just weeks into his administration, he was seeking to triple the federal education funds devoted to it. But most school districts had yet to integrate character education into their curriculums, partly out of confusion about what it was and how to teach it. In New York City, where schools were dizzying blends of cultures, languages, and religions, some principals were understandably skittish about preaching any one set of values.

Donna, however, fervently believed that it was part of her job to nourish her students' respect for themselves and one another.

Success for All had a character-education component called
"Getting Along Together," which teachers were expected to
weave into reading and other lessons. Students who physically
or verbally hurt each other had to follow a "Peace Path" through
a series of steps to conflict resolution; the class councils that
Donna was supposed to hold once a week were another part of
the program. She loved the idea of "Getting Along Together"—
by January, her teacher's guide for the program was heavily un-
derlined and full of tiny Post-its—but she rarely had time to use
it properly. Since it was usually only two students at a time who
misbehaved in a way that called for the Peace Path—hitting or
name-calling, typically—she could not devote enough attention
to leading them through the process. The rest of the class would
get too restless.

The way Donna saw it, Martin Luther King, Jr.'s birthday
was the perfect opportunity to teach the importance of respect,
kindness, and courage to the whole class at once, with no trans-
gression having triggered the lesson. So on the fifth day of the
new year, she gathered her students in the reading corner for a
picture-book biography of King. Often Donna's students mocked
subjects that were supposed to be serious, so she was surprised
and pleased at the emotional way that they reacted to King's as-
sassination. Afterwards, she suggested they talk about what
happened to King and how it made them feel.

"Sad," Nicole offered.

"I want to bust that guy up," said Shane, referring to the as-
sassin, James Earl Ray. Then Christopher, who had been quiet
as he sat at Donna's feet, raised his hand.

"My mommy got shot and killed," he said, his voice clear and
steady as a bell.

Donna suddenly felt cold all over. She had not seen Christopher's mother since school started again, but that was not un-

usual—the boy's stepfather usually picked him up. Nobody from the main office had said a word about Christopher this week, but it was possible that nobody had bothered to inform the school.

"Oh, Christopher," she said, her voice quavering slightly. "Tell me what happened."

"She got shot in the arm and she died," Christopher said, as blandly as if reciting a sentence from the Success for All books. All of his classmates were now staring at him, mouths open.

Donna beckoned Christopher and when he stood up, she took him onto her lap and murmured, "I'm so sorry," as the other students curiously looked on. Christopher squirmed and looked as if he'd rather be back on the floor.

Donna let him go and tried to continue the lesson, but her heart was pounding and her breath coming too fast. She asked Ruth Baptiste to take over and led Christopher into the hallway to gently ask more questions. He told her the shooting had happened in a cemetery, then went silent, his eyes darting. They returned to the classroom, where Donna called the senior guidance counselor and asked for his help.

After the counselor had taken Christopher away, Donna was still shaking and could not think straight. She left the room again, and this time started to sob. Shoulders heaving, she walked to the main office to break the news and ask the secretaries to call Christopher's home. She did not notice their skeptical looks through her tears. In the hallway, she ran into Patrick Cummings, a senior reading teacher, who listened to the story and consoled her.

"You need to pull yourself together," he said. "Your students need you, and they can't see you like this." He advised her not to mention Christopher's situation again until they knew for sure what had happened.

Donna blew her nose and splashed cold water on her face. Christopher's bad behavior often made her want to scream, but he also seemed so vulnerable—almost blank in his emotions, as if he did not know how to feel. His announcement about his mother was heartrending in its matter-of-factness.

Back in the classroom, Donna assumed a quiet tone and went on with the literacy lesson. The students had learned from the story that Martin Luther King, Jr. had had a dream. Now, back at their desks, Donna wanted them to talk and write about their own dreams for the world. After Christopher's story and her own dramatic response, she wanted to infuse the classroom with a sense of safety and well-being. The guidance counselor had brought Christopher back, and in particular, Donna wanted him to feel at ease.

Manuel said his dream was "peace and love and no guns." Jamilla's dream was for everyone to be happy; Patrick's was for everyone to be good.

"Wouldn't it be a wonderful world if everyone was good?" Donna murmured. "Wouldn't it be wonderful if all the world were peaceful and good?"

When they were finished writing their dreams, they all stood in a circle and, at Donna's request, held hands. No one, not even Curtis, resisted.

Inserting herself between Curtis and Nicole, Donna closed her eyes and wished aloud. "We wish for peace and love, and for no violence in our community," she said, glancing at Christopher to see how he was responding. His eyes were squeezed shut like his classmates'.

While the students were at lunch, Vera Pavone ducked her head in the door to say she'd called Christopher's house. "His mother answered the phone," she told Donna, eyebrows raised.

"Boy, do I feel foolish," Donna said quietly. Vera shrugged as if to say, "Next time you'll know better," and left.

When the children returned from lunch, she pulled the shades, turned off the lights, and had them rest their heads on their desks before the afternoon literacy lesson began. She brought out the music box that Julian had given her for Christmas, wound its base, and let it play a warped version of "Für Elise," a fitting accompaniment to a day that already felt ominous and surreal. How could she have misread the situation? Donna vividly remembered visiting P.S. 92 during her summer training and having several children announce to her, seemingly apropos of nothing, that they had heard gunfire in the night. Had it really happened, she wondered now, or did they know enough about the stereotypes attributed to their neighborhood to put on a show for visitors?

She was determined to salvage as much as she could of the morning's lesson. When the music stopped, the only sound in the classroom was Donna's chalk tap-tapping against the blackboard as she wrote the learning objective for the lesson. *L.O.: Students will discuss and write about M.L.K.'s values.*

"Who remembers what some of M.L.K.'s values were?" she said as they slowly raised their heads. "Who remembers what Ms. Moffett said? Did he believe in violence, or nonviolence?"

Christopher was the first to raise his hand. "Nonviolence," he said.

"Nonviolence, excellent. Let's write n-o-n-v-i-o-l-e-n-c-e." She went to the closet that held the contraband toys and pulled out a small red plastic gun. Now she had the class's full attention.

"Someone brought this gun way back in September," she said. "Who remembers what Ms. Moffett said?"

"You're not keeping it," Stefanie said.

"No guns in school," added Melissa, who was still silent and glum most days.

Donna drew a crude gun on the board, circled it and put a slash through it. She passed the toy gun around the room and the boys and Tasha grew excited, pulling its trigger. Christopher held onto it the longest, his eyes jumping between the gun and his teacher.

"Any other M.L.K. values, Shane?" Donna asked, calling on one of the boys who had eagerly shot off the gun.

"No violence and have peace and quiet," Shane said. Donna drew a peace sign on the board and the students squinted at it, trying to copy it into their notebooks.

"It looks like an upside-down *Y*," said Manette, the girl with the headscarf, in a rare moment of clarity. Manette was an odd child—enthusiastic, but with a short attention span and a habit of leaving her seat to wander aimlessly about the classroom.

Melissa, uncharacteristically engaged, said that another of M.L.K.'s values was love, and Donna wrote it on the board and drew a heart next to it. She took out a bag of pink and red cardboard hearts about the size of the children's hands, which she had bought on her last trip to the giant teacher supply store in downtown Brooklyn.

"Ms. Moffett is going to give you a heart. When you look at this, you can think about how much Ms. Moffett loves you. We should think about love every day. Now who wants to tape their heart in their notebook?"

The girls happily affixed their hearts to the covers of their notebooks; Curtis taped his to his forehead and the other boys followed suit.

After what had happened earlier, Donna thought the lesson

important enough to supersede math. The children were unusually attentive, perhaps eager to regain equilibrium after Christopher's frightening claim and Donna's reaction to it. She asked Briella if she remembered what Martin Luther King, Jr. said to people who wanted to use violence. Briella, the class ham, went to the front of the room and put her hands on her hips. "M.L.K. said 'If y'all wanna fight, just go somewhere else. You should leave each other alone.'"

There was a round of applause, then Donna asked who remembered what had happened to Rosa Parks, "the woman we read about who was riding a bus." Nicole raised her hand.

"The lady was tired and then the driver of the bus said go sit in the back and she didn't and then he called the police on her," she said in one breath. Donna was impressed that they vividly remembered the Rosa Parks story she had read them earlier in the week.

"When the police arrested Rosa Parks, was that fair?" she asked.

"Noooooo," Nicole cried, frowning.

After the bathroom break, Patrick walked up to the blackboard and embraced his teacher. "I love you," he said. Minutes later, Jamilla handed Donna a piece of notebook paper with "Lov You" written in pink crayon. Manette and Stefanie ran up and hugged her, and Manette dreamily murmured, "Mommy." Manette had called her that before, as had Stefanie. It bothered Donna, but she had to admit it also felt good.

Her love lesson over, Donna passed out Xeroxed worksheets that said in bold letters over a picture of a rainbow, "He had a dream; So do I!" There were lines at the bottom where the students could write their dreams. Donna was hoping that she could use these essays for her next bulletin board. As she gave instructions for the writing assignment, Curtis, who had been weathering all the mushy talk with surprising equanimity, slipped back into Curtis mode.

"Why are you so loud and you can't be quiet for one minute?" he burst out at Donna, an irritated look on his face.

She went around the room to see what each student planned to write on her or his worksheet, and found that this time around they were no longer focused on peace and harmony. Stefanie said her dream was to be beautiful.

"Except you know what, Stefanie? Let me tell you something," Donna said. "You don't have to dream about being beautiful because you're already beautiful, sweetheart." She then called on Manette, who said her dream was "to be cute," and then tried Jamilla, who said her dream was "to look beautiful."

"M.L.K. didn't say, 'When I grow up I want to be a handsome man,'" Donna said. "He said, 'I want to help people, I want the world to be fair.'"

She asked Curtis his dream, and he said, "I hope when all the children grow up they'll be as good as M.L.K., Jr." Manuel said his dream was "for people to be nice and no burglars." On his first day in her classroom, Manuel had told Donna that a burglar had tried to break into his house in the Bronx when he, his mother, and his brother were there.

"I remember the story you told me about the burglar coming to your house," Donna said.

"Yeah, but he didn't get inside," Manuel said, his eyes as serious as ever. "The police came and arrested him."

The rest of the day was a wash academically, although the aura of generosity and righteousness lingered up until the last period, when the students went with their coats and backpacks to the computer lab down the hall. Donna let the students color the rainbows on their "I have a dream" worksheets long after the literacy period should have ended. She gave them each a candy cane with reindeer antlers made of pipe cleaners, leftovers from the holiday party she had before the break.

They had skipped math completely, and instead of social studies, she wrote ten words on the blackboard and had the students copy them into their notebooks. Ad-libbing, she called each student up to spell a word, handing them the pointer and letting them tap each letter as they spelled. In keeping with the spirit of the day, they all followed instructions politely, saying "thank you" when Donna handed them the pointer. Either the spirit of Martin Luther King, Jr. was enveloping her classroom that day, or the presence of Manuel, Angelique, and Monique was beginning to change the dynamic of the class.

The peace was not shattered until 1:30, as the students hoisted their chairs onto their desks and lined up to go to computer lab. Patrick, who had been working cheerfully next to Manuel all afternoon, said something under his breath as he strode to the door. Manuel's face crumpled and he ran to Donna and pulled on her sleeve. "Ms. Moffett," he whimpered, "Patrick called me 'fat boy.'"

Donna was disappointed in Patrick, who was one of her favorites. He had boldly professed his love for her in front of the others and said his dream was to love the whole world. How could he be guilty of such an offense, especially today? She beckoned the boy from the line and asked if Manuel's accusation was true. When Patrick nodded, she sent the two boys to the back of the room to make up. Though Patrick apologized three times, Manuel kept shaking his head and saying, "I'm not a fat boy, I'm a big boy," as if to convince himself. Donna found it disorienting that a child who had apparently survived domestic

violence and an attempted robbery could get so upset about another child's teasing. Yet she, too, cringed at this small injustice,
because it had happened on her watch. And she could not prevent it from happening again.

.   .   .

For students who did act polite and respectful, Donna had invented a new reward just before Christmas that was already as
coveted as stickers and apple juice. Once or twice a week, she
chose two students to eat lunch with her in the classroom, based
on how many checkmarks for good behavior they had racked up.
To the students, it was a welcome refuge from the chaotic cafeteria and playground, where school aides yelled at them through
bullhorns and older classmates often teased or bullied them. A
few of the boys preferred the playground, but even Curtis
seemed eager for a chance to stay upstairs and be fussed over.

For Donna, the experience was equally valuable: If the children were game, she used the forty minutes to chat about their
lives outside school, sometimes gaining good clues. Usually she
just asked a question or two at the beginning: What had happened at home lately? What did they do after school yesterday?
Often it would evolve into a conversation between the two children, which itself revealed more than Donna could ever learn
while supervising twenty students at once.

One day not long after the Martin Luther King, Jr. lesson,
Nicole and Tasha were tapped for lunch. Donna picked Nicole
less to reward her good behavior—that was nothing new—than
because some of the other girls, Jamilla in particular, had been
calling her "ugly" and "baby" and making fun of her too-big uniform. A month had passed since the Christmas break, yet she
still seemed sad and out of sorts. Tasha had not been nearly as

well-behaved as Nicole—she still asked to go to the nurse at least once a day, and often brought forbidden toys and candy to class—but Donna thought she needed some positive attention, especially given her precarious housing situation.

The two girls went to the cafeteria with the rest of the class to get lunch—dried-out hamburgers, soggy Tater Tots and carrots, and warm chocolate milk—then got escorted back upstairs by their teacher, who bought the same lunch in solidarity.

Before they could tear open their plastic silverware packets, Nicole stuck out each of her hands and suggested that they pray.

"I hope nobody dies, because I like them," she said, eyes squeezed shut. Tasha nodded in assent, then reached for her hamburger. Nicole, clearly relishing her small, unthreatening audience, continued.

"Briella said the chocolate milk has doo-doo in it," she said. "She said if you give God your middle finger, he'll kick you out of heaven."

"Yeah, it's true," Tasha chimed in. "It's a curse. It means the F-word."

"Enough," Donna told them, and said that they should eat their carrots. They chewed in silence for a minute.

"God died for us already," Nicole said, looking expectantly at her teacher. Donna, an agnostic, was not sure how to respond and nodded. Several of her students were from deeply religious families; on Mondays, when Donna asked how everyone had spent their weekend, many mentioned church.

"I don't like the devil," Tasha said. "The devil is mean."

Eager to change the subject, Donna asked if Tasha and her mom were still living temporarily with her grandmother. In fact, Tasha said, they had moved again that week and were now living with cousins.

"We was going to rent an apartment, but someone took our

money and won't give it back," she said. "If Mommy don't find an apartment, we moving to Florida."

Donna asked where Tasha's daddy was—he was one of the only fathers whom she had never seen. Although Tasha had mentioned him, he had never picked her up from school and he had not come to her parent-teacher conference. Tasha said that her father lived in Queens, with her grandmother.

"He don't take me out much," she added. "I wish he'd come take me out more."

Judging by the pained look on Tasha's face and the details she'd provided—so different from Christopher's weird tale of the cemetery shooting and his casual way of telling it—Donna guessed that the circumstances she had described were real. Yet she was careful not to react in the visceral way she had with Christopher. The news of her outburst earlier that month had circulated around the school, and some of her colleagues had gently mocked her gullibility.

"These children are starving for attention," one had told her. "You have to take everything they say with a grain of salt, because they tell these tall tales all the time, especially the little ones."

But even as Donna vowed never again to respond to a child's allegations in the panicked way she had treated Christopher that morning, she also promised herself that she would never dismiss any claim out of hand.

Like so many of her students, Donna herself had not been so different from the "Sad Girl" in the Teaching Fellows ad as a child: forlorn, neglected, and even, at times, in harm's way. The parallels between her own childhood and that of students like Tasha and Nicole made Donna identify deeply with them and want to do things for them—such as giving up her lunch hour and empathizing with Christopher—that isolated her from her colleagues. She could not help but feel, at times like this, that it was her and her students against the world.

.   .   .

By the week of the Martin Luther King, Jr. holiday, Donna had a tickle in her throat, then a cough and a persistent headache. She tried to bolster her immune system with tincture of echinacea and hot baths, but by the time the dismissal bell rang on Tuesday, Donna felt so achy and tired that for one of the first times since she had started teaching, she left the building when the students did. Even Brenda Robertson urged Donna to skip her Brooklyn College class and go straight home to bed.

Donna was touched; she and Robertson had been trying to mend fences since their November confrontation. Donna brought Robertson coffee now and then, and Robertson made a point of praising things Donna had done.

By Thursday, Donna had a temperature of 103 and a full-blown case of pneumonia. The next week was a blur of feverish dreams, and Donna barely raised her head from her pillow. Ruth Baptiste called to report that a science teacher who did not have her own classroom was substituting. She also said that Marie Buchanan had seized the opportunity of Donna's absence to overhaul the learning centers scattered around the classroom, which she thought Donna had willfully neglected.

Donna knew that late January was a bad time to disappear. February 1, just a week away, marked the halfway point in the school year, and she had been told it was an important moment to take stock of each student's progress. Lying in bed as she recovered, she thought a lot about the students who she knew were in serious academic trouble. There was Curtis, whose artistic talents and verbal acuity made her believe he was gifted, but who could not focus on any assignment long enough to complete it. There was Trevor, who still babbled like a three-year-old and was nowhere near reading. He often seemed to want to succeed, calling Donna over to look at his notebook and help him write words. Yet during a recent writing assignment, Trevor had scribbled all over his paper and thrown it on the floor, whining in his baby voice, "I can't do it, I doh-wanna wite."

Trevor had been saying stupid things for attention—when Donna asked him for the answer to a question, he'd say something nonsensical like "Poop" or "Pancake." Though some of his classmates laughed, Stefanie, whose disobedience had confounded Donna in the fall, had reproached Trevor.

"That's not funny!" she'd told him, glaring. Unfortunately, Stefanie was absent so often that her performance had not improved with her behavior.

Melissa and Manette were also "promotion in doubt," as the lingo went. While Donna could assume Melissa's problems were partly due to her new baby brother, Manette remained an enigma. Her mother had come for a conference in November, and had said in broken English that she was a home healthcare aide. She said that she had been a teacher in her native Haiti, and promised to help Manette improve.

But while Manette was one of the most enthusiastic children in the class—often the first to raise her hand—she seemed totally clueless most of the time. When Donna had asked her what day it was one December morning, Manette had looked out the window at lightly falling snow and answered, "July." She had a hard time paying attention and would goof off instead, peering inside Briella's desk or mock-hitting Cindy or getting out of her seat to give Monique a hug. Donna had recently checked in with Manette's kindergarten teacher, who told her that Manette had behaved the exact same way in her class.

But the student Donna feared for the most was Cindy, the Puerto Rican girl who was absent at least once a week and who, when she did come to school, had to be prodded to even pick up a pencil. Donna also felt guiltiest about Cindy, who, unlike Curtis and some of the other stragglers, did not have any winning traits that might have inspired Donna to bond with her.

Cindy still hit and stole from other children, threw tantrums if Donna took away a toy she had sneaked in, and seemed to have no interest whatsoever in learning. She reveled in bathroom breaks and lunch. She was at her most energetic and engaged when Donna handed out treats, and would often ask for two. Although her mother had been in the classroom a lot because of Cindy's separation anxiety, Donna had barely spoken to her because they didn't share a language.

She already felt certain that Cindy needed to repeat first grade, and she was bent on making it happen. After all, the girl had skipped kindergarten. No thought had been given to the fact that Cindy did not know her alphabet when she had been placed in Room 218.

The way Donna saw it, Cindy's problems were so complex that it was useless for her, a new teacher, to try to solve them. If she gave Cindy the attention she needed, many other students would suffer. Why put too much effort into one whom she probably could not help anyway, at the expense of others whom she likely could?

Donna was emboldened by the fact that a year earlier, the Board of Ed had adopted a strict new policy theoretically ending "social promotion"—the longstanding practice of promoting students with failing grades for the sake of their self-esteem. By mid-February, every teacher in the system had to determine which students were likely to have to repeat their grade, and send warning letters to their parents. Identifying academic stragglers in February helped the system plan for summer school and gave parents ample warning, so they would have fewer grounds to contest a decision to hold their child back come June.

Like so many other high-profile attempts to fix urban schools, ending social promotion was not a new idea; just another pendulum swing back from an opposite tack that had failed. In the 1980s, another New York schools chancellor, Frank Macchiarola, had started holding back thousands of fourth- and seventh-graders who did not reach a minimum score on a standardized reading test, and who failed yet again during summer school. But budget constraints kept the Board of Ed from providing remedial help to the students who had flunked, and so many were retained two years in a row.

In 1990, another chancellor, Joseph Fernandez, canceled the cost-prohibitive program, allowing tens of thousands of children to be promoted each year without mastering basic skills. Fernandez believed that holding students back eroded their self-esteem. Now, in 2000, social promotion had been outlawed once again, and veterans of the system, familiar with the vagaries of city budgets and short lives of so many trendy education reforms, could not help but be skeptical.

The idea of ending social promotion was catching on again elsewhere, too, a product of the Republican revolution that Newt Gingrich had started in the 1990s. It reflected the get-tough mentality that had led to overhauls of the nation's criminal justice and welfare systems. And, like efforts to cut the welfare rolls and send low-level offenders to jail en masse, it was drawing bipartisan support: President Bill Clinton had called for ending social promotion in his 1999 State of the Union address. According to the "no excuses" philosophy that politicians were embracing, advancing children who had not mastered the basics of their grade not only rewarded them unfairly and enabled them to keep failing without consequence, but also slowed down the higher-achieving students with whom they were promoted. On its face, this logic was tough to take issue with; the public and even the teachers' unions were endorsing it.

But when politicians grandly announced plans to end social promotion, few envisioned the blunt realities that would eventually result. If school systems held true to their word and retained every failing student, some grades would have far more children than they were supposed to, which meant schools would have to hire more teachers, find more classroom space, and buy more books. In places like New York, Chicago, and Los Angeles, that could cost hundreds of millions of dollars, a significant chunk of budgets that had already been spread impossibly thin. Some students would be held back repeatedly, so that seventh-grade classrooms might be full of apathetic seventeen-year-olds—a scenario that would hardly benefit the twelve-year-olds there for the first time. A strict retention policy might work well in suburban districts, where smaller groups of students were held back and it would be easier to give each the intensive help she or he needed in summer school and beyond. But suburban parents were more apt than their poor urban counterparts to fight grade retention, and particularly the idea of failing a child based on a single high-stakes test, as stigmatizing and unfair. They demanded, and their districts found money for, tutoring and other intervention programs during the school year, so that students would not fall so far behind as to need to repeat.

This year in New York, the warning notices about summer school would be form letters written by a Board of Ed administrator—an inappropriately cold method of delivering such serious news, Donna thought. So when her fever broke, she wrote a letter to all her students' parents that she hoped would have a troop-rallying effect. She pointed out that they were halfway through the school year and said that it was time for the students to redouble their efforts, adding that she expected to see enormous leaps in the coming five months.

"Some students are internally motivated, while others need a little push or quite a bit of extra help," she wrote. "We can help more students excel."

Not that Donna was getting the kind of extra help *she* needed. To make matters worse, the Board of Ed was pressuring principals not to place students in special-education classes, which were hugely expensive and seen, often correctly, as warehouses for badly behaved black boys. On paper, the board's latest plan was to keep students with learning disabilities or chronic behavior problems in regular classrooms instead of assigning them to separate rooms for special instruction. On paper, the board planned to train all teachers in dealing with various disabilities, and assign an extra teacher or aide to classrooms with more than a few learning-disabled children. This would be a huge change from the decades-old standard of keeping New York City's 150,000 special-education students, with handicaps ranging from minor learning disabilities to severe mental retardation, separate from the general school population.

But in reality, hardly anyone was getting this new training—even as the board was telling schools to cut way back on special-ed placements. In years past, students like Manette and

Christopher might well have been sent to special-ed classes for at least part of the day. Now they were fully Donna's problem, even though they were far behind most of their classmates developmentally. Once again, the Board of Ed had adopted an admirable-sounding special-ed policy without providing the resources to ensure its success.

This, too, was happening throughout the nation, for it was now politically correct to proclaim that special education had failed too many vulnerable minority students by hiding them away in separate classrooms and seldom equipping them with the skills they would need to make it in the world.

But leaving disruptive or learning-disabled children in regular classrooms, with teachers who were too new or otherwise unskilled to give them what they needed, was a recipe for ensuring that they would languish as much as they had under the old warehousing system. The idea of keeping such children "mainstreamed," as the jargon went, was admirable, with the potential to help thousands across the country succeed each year. But if classroom teachers could not be trained to work with these students while also tending to their higher-achieving peers, and if specialists could not be in their classrooms to help—again, an investment of several hundred million dollars a year in large school districts—this was just another impressive-sounding, sickeningly empty plan.

·   ·   ·

On Thursday the 25th, when Donna had been out sick for a full week, a friend stopped by the school to pick up some materials for her. Her friend brought her an extra surprise: a folder full of lovingly made get-well cards. Their drawings and messages suggested the students missed her intensely, and that some even feared she might not come back. For children who craved consistency, their worries were understandable.

Then, that Friday, Ruth Baptiste called again with some jolting news: Christopher had been pulled from Donna's class. Dakota Reyes, the instructional specialist who had been dropping in every few weeks, had told Diana Rahmaan and Brenda Robertson that Donna could not handle the boy, and that he would confound even a veteran teacher.

Reyes and Robertson had already told Donna that Christopher might be moved, a proposition that made her feel more relief than guilt. Donna suspected that the Martin Luther King, Jr. incident, and her reaction to it, had speeded Christopher's removal. But she accepted Robertson's explanation: that the time was right to move him to another first-grade classroom because that class had just lost a student, and because Donna, who had been assigned a fourth new student while she was out sick, had more than ever on her plate.

Although Donna was once again missing a lot of school, her relationship with P.S. 92 while she was out sick demonstrated how much had changed since October. She felt so much more a part of the school now, and more confident of her place there. When she finally returned to P.S. 92 the following Monday, after being gone for a third of the month, her students smothered her with hugs and kisses.

As she asked how they were, Donna wondered whether Christopher was feeling punished or disoriented, and how his new classmates were treating him. She talked herself into believing what colleagues had told her—that young children are remarkably adaptive—and took comfort in knowing he was with a more experienced teacher.

It did not help, though, that Donna had seen Jamal, the troublemaker who had been sent back to kindergarten in November, in the lunchroom one day. He had been sitting alone, and when Donna had asked whose class he was in, he had looked up, expressionless, and said, "I don't know."

Her heart had not stopped aching that day, but given the choice, she admitted now, she would not have had Jamal or Christopher back.

The new boy was Franklin Aiken, who Vera Pavone said had just arrived from Trinidad and was living with his young aunt. He was taller than the others, with a huge smile and no front teeth. He eagerly joined the swarm of children who thronged Donna when she reappeared that Monday morning, despite having no idea who she was.

Manette, one of the five students in danger of failing, seemed especially happy about Donna's return. On Donna's second morning back, she came to class with a large bag, placed it on her desk, and looked at Donna meaningfully as she sat down. When Donna asked what was inside, Manette smiled but acted shy, whispering to Stefanie, her neighbor.

"It's for you, Ms. Moffett!" Stefanie announced.

Donna asked Manette if she could look inside the bag, and when Manette nodded, she reached in and pulled out a shoebox with a mismatched top and bottom. Its contents were mystifying: a few potato chips and pieces of popcorn, and a blank piece of paper.

"My goodness, Manette," Donna stammered. "Is this a gift?"

Manette nodded, looking proud.

"Well thank you very much, sweetheart!" She had thanked the students for their get-well cards the day before, and now, she figured, Manette had decided to bring in another token of affection. But the incident only deepened Donna's concern about Manette's capabilities. She wrote a note to the school guidance counselors that afternoon, asking that they evaluate Manette as soon as possible.

CHAPTER SIX

Since she could not peer into her students' lives, Donna invented the crudest of crystal balls. It was a coffee can full of Popsicle sticks, each inscribed with a student's name, and four soup cans, all labeled with an adjective: happy, sad, angry, sick. She called it the Mood Monitor.

When Donna took attendance in the morning, she invited the students to put their sticks in the can whose label best matched their respective moods. Simplistic, yes, but at least it gave her a hint of what to expect from day to day. "Sick" was a surprisingly popular choice, especially with Tasha and Melissa. Curtis chose "angry" most mornings, with a glowering look, but refused to explain why. Donna guessed that he didn't know, or at least couldn't articulate the reason.

So much about these children was still unexplained, even after ninety days in their close company. Lacking the facts, Donna made grim assumptions about their idiosyncrasies: Stefanie complained of stomachaches several times a week because she did not eat enough at home, she guessed. Tasha asked to go to the nurse's office when she appeared perfectly healthy because she was bored, her attention span nonexistent. Donna had no idea why Curtis obsessively drew monsters with tentacles and fangs instead of writing letters and words, though she knew that at the very least, he was exposed to inappropriate television. A connoisseur of horror movies at six, he talked enthusiastically about slasher films like *Scream* and *Evil Dead*, and the TV show *Buffy the Vampire Slayer*.

Cindy was another mystery. She had missed thirty-one days of school—a third of the year so far—and was tardy on another twenty-seven. Rumors about Cindy weighed heavily on Donna: Was she really the youngest of thirteen children? Donna had told her supervisors how worried she was about the girl's absences, and they had assigned a truancy officer to her case after Christmas. But Donna had not heard any updates.

So far, some of the best clues about her students came from the battered "record tin" on the windowsill near her desk. There was one in every elementary school classroom in New York City, with files guarding the vital statistics of each student. While most of the files in Donna's record tin were thin, they at least contained the standard questionnaire that parents fill out when they register their children for any New York public school. Besides the student's date of birth, address, and phone number, it asks where the student and his or her parents were born. Thanks only to the record tin, Donna knew that Stefanie had been born in Panama, Manette in Haiti, and Trevor right at Kings County Hospital, though his mother was from Guyana. The only mothers who were U.S.-born were Briella's, Curtis's, and Tasha's.

Donna knew from her lunches with the children that some parents worked two jobs—Jamilla's mother, for example, cleaned offices and worked in a bank—and that others had huge extended families to care for. Some took boarders in their small, crowded apartments to help pay the rent. Many mothers, like Manette's and Stefanie's, struggled with English.

Occasionally, Donna had gleaned darker hints about the hardships her students faced. Stefanie, whose increasingly good behavior had won her several lunches with Donna, announced over a tray of chicken nuggets and mushy carrots one Monday that her parents had fought over the weekend. "My mommy said, 'Get out, get out,' and she called the policeman," she told Donna breathlessly. On several recent mornings, Stefanie had clutched her stomach and resisted leaving the classroom for Success for All, begging to stay with the teacher she knew best.

.   .   .

Donna had met Stefanie's mother only once, on the first day of school. The woman had skipped her parent-teacher conference in November, though when she belatedly returned Stefanie's report card, she wrote at the bottom: "Please, I promise you that Stefanie will come better. If you get any further problem wit her please contact me." Yet the child had continued to miss school—she had been absent eighteen days so far, the worst record after Cindy's.

As if there were not enough questions, two more students joined the class in early February. Since September, Donna had gained six students and lost six others, part of the constant, chaotic churn of students in and out of New York City classrooms over the course of each year. Michelle Griffin had moved from the island of Jamaica, where, according to the registration card her mother had filled out, Michelle had attended school for only three months. Mariah Jenkins, who spelled as perfectly as Manuel and wrote as expressively as Angelique, came from another school in Brooklyn. Michelle was boisterous and affectionate, Mariah painfully shy, saying nothing but quiet yeses and nos. She drew intricate, dreamy pictures, usually of herself and her baby brother on swings or in gardens. The records that would come from Mariah's old school over a month later would show she had attended six schools since kindergarten.

Incredibly, the photographs Donna had taken of the parents on the first day of school remained her best information about these strangers her students went home to every day. The pictures were as familiar to her now as the little squares that represented days in her lesson-planning book and the constant scraping of wooden chairs against her blue-tile floor. But the polite smiles that filled the album labeled "Family" answered none of the worrisome questions that filled Donna's mind late at night as she graded homework, mulled the events of the day, and waited for sleep.

.   .   .

Other teachers at P.S. 92 and throughout the city called parents occasionally or even once a week to report bad behavior, academic problems, and bits of good news. Many, like Jim Raffel, her teaching fellow colleague, had bought cell phones just to stay in touch with parents and spent hours doing so after school or on weekends. But Donna had decided early on that she could not afford a cell phone, and her few attempts at calling parents had not worked any miracles. Since she could not make outside calls from the old phone in Room 218, Donna had to use the lines in the main office, which had the feel of Grand Central Station even after school let out. Teachers competed for the office phones after 3:00, and there was sometimes a wait. Calling in the late afternoon was often useless, anyway, because most parents were at work and their jobs typically did not allow access to a phone.

Donna had no will to call parents from home at night, because she was consumed with figuring out how to keep the next day from dissolving into chaos. There was at least an hour's preparation for Success for All, rehearsing the script and every segment of the lesson. Preparing for math, social studies, and science sometimes took another two or three.

While some of her colleagues felt that phoning had helped them bond with parents and improve some children's behavior or academic performance, others, including Jim Raffel, were finding calls home an exercise in frustration. Some parents openly resented Jim's calls about their children's rudeness or failure to do homework, acting defensive or even hanging up on him. Others were apologetic, but offered no solution when Jim told them about a problem. If he couldn't handle a child, he was learning, chances were good that the parent couldn't, either.

Jim finally stopped calling his students' homes around midyear, after the third or fourth time that a parent promised to give her or his child a beating after he reported bad behavior. When he told Donna the story, she had a similar one to share. Trevor's stepfather had come in for a conference, and had been upset to hear that Trevor had not yet learned all his letters. Trevor had come to class the next morning with a small welt on his cheek— as if someone had hit him with a belt, Donna worried. Trevor denied being hit when she asked him, but Donna still feared that his stepfather had lashed out at him, and wondered along with Jim how many well-meaning conversations with parents put the children of P.S. 92 in harm's way.

By February, Donna had settled into a more old-fashioned

and, she hoped, less threatening way of communicating: sending her students home with dozens of notes, written in teacher-perfect script and signed with a heart or smiley face. Some were simply celebratory, telling parents how pleased she was with their child's work or personality, while others took a worried tone. Sending notes, Donna could at least imagine that the parents appreciated her concern and were willing to improve their children's behavior or work with them on spelling, math, or reading. But by now, the silence that usually followed her notes—and her lack of progress with the children in question— forced Donna to admit that notes seldom worked. They were like messages in bottles, tossed into the waves with a wish or prayer, but with no guarantee that they would ever be read.

After her own extended absence in January, Donna had sent notes home with Stefanie, Tasha, Shakeela, Trevor, and Cindy, pointing out how often they had been late or absent, and warning that they could be held back as a result. She asked that the parents sign and return the notes, but two weeks later, only Shakeela's mother—who had taught her daughter to read so well— had done so.

.   .   .

Melissa, though she had her good days, continued to vex. She would stare morosely at the floor when Donna called on her. But Stefanie was always shooting up her hand—even if, as was usually the case, she had no idea what to say. Stefanie was often the first to reach the story corner and would sit as close as possible to Donna, eyes dancing, while it sometimes took three promptings to get Melissa there at all.

One day, when Donna had told everyone to assume the "active listening" position—hands clasped, spine straight, eyes on the teacher—Melissa had been the only one to refuse. She had kept slouching and drawing in her notebook, even as Donna asked her with increasing irritation to obey.

It was easier to love Stefanie than Melissa—perhaps that helped explain Stefanie's constant enthusiasm. Like Curtis, the other lovable troublemaker, Stefanie could surely sense Donna's fondness even when Donna was punishing her. Back in the fall, when Stefanie acted up regularly, Donna had even laughed a few times in the middle of scolding her.

Melissa, on the other hand, rarely elicited a spontaneous laugh or smile from Donna. Lately, Donna had tried to smile encouragingly when she called on Melissa, and to lavish praise when the girl even partly followed directions. But those gestures were somewhat forced—she simply did not feel the same affinity for Melissa as for Stefanie.

Donna held out a lot of hope for Stefanie. She was one of Donna's favorites despite her absences, her slowness to recognize even the simplest words, and her outbursts, which happened less often these days but still astounded Donna with their ferocity. Compared with Melissa, who was more innately capable, Stefanie was a firecracker—in the best of ways.

In children so young, motivation probably has a lot to do with feeling embraced by the adults around them. But it was hard for Donna to love problem students unconditionally when she had so many deficiencies as a teacher. Her impatience with Melissa had taken its toll; the girl was wary of her. This was a troubling, though entirely typical, aspect of teaching: It is human nature to be drawn to some personalities and annoyed by others, and every teacher through the ages has faced the dilemma of liking some students better than others. Guidance from the school or

Melissa's parents would have helped enormously—if Melissa had been born into affluence, her parents might have hired a private psychologist to treat her depression, a specialist to diagnose any learning disabilities, and a tutor to help with academic problems. They might have insisted on extra help for Melissa, which in a top-flight school might mean working one-on-one a few times a week with a teacher specially trained to address her specific weaknesses.

But schools like P.S. 92 had too many other pressing problems to provide such services. Parents were often too busy with day-to-day survival, or just intimidated by the school bureaucracy. So students like Melissa, who were quietly wrestling with some mysterious problem or other but whose behavior was not out of control, remained misunderstood and neglected.

In mid-February, Donna wrote a plaintive note to Melissa's mother, trying hard not to sound the least bit angry or accusatory: "I am very concerned about Melissa. Is there anything going on with her that we should know about? I believe she has abilities but she seems to not apply herself. When you are free, we should get together. What date would be good for you to meet after 3:00? I'd like to help."

But the note went unanswered, and Donna's disappointment mixed with anger.

·   ·   ·

One of the only parents who stopped by Room 218 regularly was Curtis's mom, the talkative, tough-acting Liana. She looked like a teenager, with long shaggy hair, a wardrobe of T-shirts and jeans, and keys hanging from a cord around her neck. Liana hung around P.S. 92 a lot and knew just about everyone, especially the teachers' aides who, like her, were young and gossipy and lived in the neighborhood. She was the first to sign up when Donna sought helpers for field trips or parties, and she frequently stopped Donna in the hallway to ask how Curtis was doing.

But Donna's relationship with Liana was proving that hands-on parents could be just as frustrating as those who never showed up. Unlike most of the parents Donna had encountered, Liana had opinions about everything that happened to her son at P.S. 92. And they were seldom rosy. Take, for example, when Irwin Kurz, the district superintendent, had visited Donna's classroom in October and observed Curtis calling out inappropriate comments about blood and scary movies. Kurz had recommended that the boy be screened for learning disabilities and perhaps placed in special education. But Liana had been livid, and had refused to have him tested. Donna had been quietly relieved at Liana's belligerence: She'd heard that special-ed classes were often a dumping ground for black and Hispanic boys with behavior problems, and she thought Curtis was too gifted and creative to end up there.

But Liana had then turned on Donna, blaming her for Curtis's lack of academic progress. She knew that Donna was completely inexperienced and seemed to resent that her son, if he really needed extra help, had been stuck with a novice. Liana had complained at least once to the principal and tried to have him moved to another class, but Diana Rahmaan had resisted.

Donna's superiors had warned her not to tell Liana that Curtis was gifted. It could backfire later, they said, if Curtis's performance did not improve and other teachers wanted to screen him for learning disabilities. So Donna walked a fine line with Liana, saying how much she loved Curtis but that he was not living up to her expectations, behaviorally or academically. Liana remained guarded around her, appreciating her interest in Curtis but often looking at her skeptically, as if suspecting Donna of ulterior motives.

After the holidays, Donna had made a proposal that Liana seemed to like: She would work with Curtis one-on-one before school twice a week, helping him practice writing and reading. It would mean leaving home at 6:30 a.m. instead of 7:00, when she barely made it out the door as it was. But Curtis, like Stefanie, was such a compelling case, with so much potential, that Donna could not resist. More than anything, she wanted Curtis to be reading by June.

Liana acted grateful for the offer, beaming and allowing Donna a rare compliment: She said that Curtis had come home one day and announced, "I want to live with Ms. Moffett for six months."

. . .

As Valentine's Day approached, Donna thought she would try to lure parents to Room 218 using one of her strongest skills from her old job: planning a lavish party. She designed a florid invitation, covered in hearts and entreating parents to "come share the love," for her students to take home. But first she ran the invitation by Diana Rahmaan, since she had been warned against holding too many parties.

Rahmaan approved the party but sent the invitation back with a note asking Donna to tone it down; she thought the gushy language might make some parents uncomfortable. Perhaps because the invitation could not be as creative as Donna liked, she made sure that her outfit on Valentine's Day was: She showed up to school in a cherry-red suit, red tights, red socks adorned with flowers, a red apron, and dangly red heart earrings.

Donna's colleagues seemed half-amused, half-exasperated as she walked beamingly into the main office that morning, inviting all the secretaries and any teacher she saw to stop by her classroom for the big event.

Brenda Robertson had insisted that Donna delay the festivities until 1:30, but the students were so restless and excited that she stopped teaching around 1:00. She had them clean their desks with wet paper towels and get their backpacks out of the closet so they would be ready for dismissal at 2:20. As they worked, she lined some desks in the back of the room with red paper tablecloths and laid out the foods she had carefully chosen: cranberry juice, cookies with red sprinkles, and pizza.

Some children had contributed treats: Tasha brought a bag of ketchup-flavored potato chips, and Briella brought pink cupcakes that she had made with her mother. Donna imagined them in their kitchen together, Briella standing on a chair with a mixing spoon, and wondered if Briella's happiness and good grades were a result of this closeness.

Donna had stayed up late the night before, writing out valentines to each student. Most of the girls carefully tucked them away, and most of the boys abandoned them as the party got underway. Liana arrived at 1:30 and set about etching hearts on the students' faces with the red face paint Donna had brought, clowning around with them but largely ignoring Donna. Michelle's mother also came, but she sat shyly on the sidelines and watched. When Donna tried to engage her in conversation, she spoke in halting, uncomfortable English.

They were the only parents to show up.

The students had relished this brief break from academics, but inviting parents to a midday party had proved as useless as sending them notes. Donna would have to find other ways to connect, ones that would require considerably more energy than she had been willing to spend so far. One intriguing idea, which Michael Bloomberg, the Republican mayoral candidate hoping to succeed Rudy Giuliani, had proposed, was that teachers should visit all their students' homes at least once a year. A few California school districts had experimented with "teacher house calls" to promising effect—an evaluation of the program found it resulted in more parental involvement and fewer discipline problems—but it would not take off in New York just yet. While some teachers were bold and energetic enough to occasionally knock on the doors of their most difficult students, trying to disarm and engage their parents outside the school environment that intimidated so many of them, the union would dismiss Bloomberg's plan as dangerous and logistically daunting. Even if Donna had ventured to the homes of Manette, Stefanie, or Cindy, language barriers would have kept her from having heart-to-hearts with their mothers, though the gesture might have moved them.

Donna did not think about her latest failure as the party wound down, though. Nicole lost her first tooth biting into a cookie, and when she cried at the blood, Donna swooped down to comfort her and offer a special envelope for the tooth to go home in.

Then, she brought out one last treat: her collection of heart-shaped boxes, gathered over two decades and normally displayed on tables and shelves around her apartment. Two were made of china, and painted with delicate flowers. The others, each smaller than the one before, were of wood. In them she kept heart-shaped jewelry—earrings, a pin and bracelet, and a locket from her mother—and relics like her high school ring and the tiny hospital bracelet that her father had worn when he was born.

A year earlier, the Donna who did not keep much more than a plant on her desk at Flemming, Zulack could not have imagined bringing her fragile heart collection to a chaotic classroom, and letting six-year-olds press the boxes to their lips and cheeks. But now, these trinkets that she had tended so carefully seemed perfect for show and tell—a part of herself to share with these children who had real hearts pumping inside them.

.   .   .

On a Wednesday afternoon in March, Donna hunched over one of the little wooden tables in 218, surrounded by heaps of worksheets and notebooks. It was report card time again. She wanted her comments to be especially thoughtful for this second round, even if some parents never gave them a glance.

Only one more marking period remained—one last chance to push the so-so students, like Melissa and Nicole, over a few humps, and to toss the real stragglers, like Cindy and Manette, some kind of life raft. Donna marked Manette "good" for showing initiative and "satisfactory" in three categories: math, showing an interest in reading, and knowing science facts and concepts.

"Manette shows a great deal of initiative and she tries to do her work," she wrote in her signature purple ink. "She clearly wants to learn, participate, and do well. I am very concerned that Manette needs a great deal of help so she recognizes all letters of the alphabet as well as sight words. Tutoring and counseling would be helpful and are strongly suggested." Maybe saying that colleagues shared her concern about Manette would add heft, though her attempts to get Manette evaluated for learning disabilities had so far failed.

Melissa got "satisfactory" in about half of the categories and rovement" in the rest. But Donna also marked her

ory," the lowest grade, in obeying rules and showing self-control. The girl was as sullen and unresponsive as ever, and Donna was sure that she was seriously depressed. Recently, instead of copying a homework assignment, Melissa had sketched a stick figure lying on a crude square. "Me in bed," she had flatly explained.

Donna made her writing extra-small to squeeze a lot into Melissa's comment box. As with the other problem students, her comments were of the "I can't save this child on my own" variety.

"I am very concerned about Melissa," she wrote. "Her academic performance and behavior in class strongly suggest Melissa is AT RISK. Melissa is less well-behaved than she was in the fall. She calls out frequently and usually does not do her work. She seems less motivated and, while I believe she is capable, Melissa is in urgent need of additional help and support."

As an afterthought, she added: "Melissa still complains she cannot see even though we moved her right in front of the board."

Just that afternoon, Donna had scooted Melissa's chair to within feet of the blackboard when it came time to copy down the homework assignment. Most of the students had written the four sentences of instructions and ten spelling words quickly, and Donna had sent them to play in the learning centers while the stragglers poked along.

After ten minutes, Melissa had not even finished writing the requisite header—her name, school, class, and the date—at the top of her notebook page. She had stopped working constantly to stare at or listen to classmates who were buzzing around her. And she had to look back at the board between each letter, to remind herself what came next.

Fifteen minutes into the exercise, Melissa had written one sentence and started another, but got distracted and skipped to the third. When Donna pointed out the mistake and Melissa fixed it, Donna stuck a star sticker on her wrist. "See, you're such a smart girl. You make me so happy when you do your work."

Melissa finally began copying the spelling words by 1:25, but complained because other students, who had finished a half-hour earlier, were walking past and blocking the board. "Scuze me!" she kept saying in frustration.

She finished at 1:32—forty-two minutes after she began. Curtis had finished only five minutes earlier; Cindy and Manette, not at all.

A math lesson should have taken place in the time that had passed. But Donna had decided to keep Melissa and the other slow writers focused on this rudimentary task and let the others tinker in the learning centers, giving herself time to clear her head. She still could not handle so many different ability levels at once. So the stragglers labored over a trivial assignment that only frustrated them and made them unhappy to be in school, while the achievers were sent off to play, unsupervised and unchallenged.

.   .   .

Inexplicably, Donna had far more success with parent conferences this time around—though four students' parents had again not shown up, most of the discussions had been constructive and upbeat. The mothers of some of the most troubled kids—Stefanie and Cindy—were among the missing. And of course, they would not sign or return the report cards that Donna painstakingly prepared.

The longest and most productive session was with Melissa's mother, Rose Charles. Donna was shocked that Rose had come, since she had ignored Donna's plaintive notes for months. Rose was tall, with Melissa's almond-shaped eyes, and she spoke in broken English. At first, she was quiet and stiff as Donna described Melissa's concentration problems and sadness.

But Donna was disarming, and Rose eventually let her body relax and admitted that she, too, was worried about her daughter.

"She is spiritless," Rose murmured in her soft, lilting cadence. As she began to speak, Donna leaned forward and listened silently, picturing for the first time the life that Melissa went home to every afternoon.

Melissa was the oldest of four children in their household, Rose explained. The two youngest—a three-year-old girl and a baby born in November—were Melissa's half-siblings. The second oldest, a five-year-old boy, was mentally disabled and went to a special school.

Donna had known about the new baby, but Melissa had never mentioned her disabled brother. Listening to Rose, Donna sensed that he got an inordinate share of the household's attention.

Melissa and her brother visited their father in Queens on weekends, but his house, like theirs, was overflowing. The father had two children from his new marriage, Rose explained. Donna assumed that Melissa did not get enough attention there, either. It all helped explain her behavior, from sticking up her middle finger in the lunch line to freezing when Donna addressed her. Melissa craved attention and sought it in negative ways, but when an adult actually focused on her, she had no idea how to respond.

Rose felt guilty. She attended night school, so she was not there for Melissa many evenings. As the oldest, Melissa was expected to help with her siblings when her mother was not home, and probably got more than her share of responsibility all the time.

Donna recommended counseling, and when Rose agreed, Donna called Colleen Dewgard, a new, young guidance counselor with a sweet face and gentle touch. Dewgard came to meet Rose as the conference ended, and promised to do what she could for Melissa.

Rose grabbed Donna's hands as she was leaving, and Donna pulled her into a hug. This had been her most honest, intense exchange with a parent. She came away from it with a new, softened perspective on Melissa and her desultory ways. If only it had come six months earlier.

CHAPTER SEVEN

Winter was finally over, but the first tentative days of spring in Flatbush did little to counter the cynicism simmering in Donna. Five months at P.S. 92 had stirred in her the beginnings of disdain toward the common, sugarcoated view of inner-city teachers that she had admittedly bought into the previous year.

"Every child can learn," the George W. Bush campaign mantra that was to become the cornerstone of his education policy, echoed in Donna's mind as conflicting feelings buffeted her. She still cherished the goal of the Teaching Fellows program: to give fragile, disadvantaged children as sound an education as those born into affluence. Yet when it came to children like Cindy and Manette, Bush's oft-repeated call to end "the soft bigotry of low expectations" for poor minority students seemed willfully naïve.

As if political bromides about teaching were not enough, there were also the wildly unrealistic stereotypes that Hollywood peddled, and that the public—Donna included, until this year—swallowed whole. She had wistfully admired movies like *Dangerous Minds* and *To Sir, with Love,* which shape so many people's notions about teaching in a tough school. Their teacher-heroes were also truant officers, social workers, and fairy godparents, marching to the homes of wayward students or connecting with their parents in heartfelt, fate-changing conversations. Unfortunately for the students of Room 218, life in Flatbush was no movie and Donna no celluloid heroine. She could not live up to the impossible standards that Hollywood had established for teachers. More and more these days, she could not imagine ever doing so.

The apathy of so many parents, born of poverty so entrenched in their communities that they could see no way out, was damning. But it was not just them—the school system, elephantine, rigidly bureaucratic, and always short on funds, was just as unresponsive. The size of P.S. 92 alone—1,100 students and 200 teachers on 5 sprawling floors—all but guaranteed that many children's needs would be overlooked. Somewhere between Labor Day and Valentine's Day, Donna had lost the conviction that she could lift each and every one of her students up by June.

She had never heard back about the investigation into Cindy's truancy. Nor had the guidance counselors responded to her note about Manette and the crumb-filled box. The three counselors at P.S. 92 struggled under staggering caseloads, and puzzling but non-urgent cases like Manette's were often put on the back burner while they dealt with more glaring problems: children who had been physically or sexually abused, or who were acting so violently that their classmates were not safe.

Yet as the school failed to respond nimbly to the glaring needs of Cindy, Manette, and so many other students, it remained extraordinarily vigilant about following bureaucratic rules that Donna and other teaching fellows found pointless. The bulletin boards, for example: Why were supervisors so quick to reprimand a teacher whose board was the least bit sloppy, while taking months to answer a request for special services for a student? The emphasis was on accountability to the bureaucracy and its shallow, easily enforceable rules, not to the children whose needs were too complex for the one-size-fits-all solutions so typical of huge systems. Donna, like many of her fellow teachers, found it very sad.

.   .   .

Case in point: One morning, Marie Buchanan and Brenda Robertson had briefly entered 218 and huddled by the door, studying the walls and whispering. Success for All was just ending at 10:15 when Buchanan returned and pulled Donna aside; officials from the State Education Department were arriving any minute to walk the hallways, inspect classrooms, and observe teachers. Diana Rahmaan was out of the building at meetings, and the state had called just an hour ago to tell them about the surprise visit.

As a failing school for more than a decade, P.S. 92 was well-accustomed to outside scrutiny, including several visits a year from state bureaucrats who kept track of the school's progress or lack thereof. Clipboards in hand, they looked to see if the bathrooms had toilet paper and soap, and if the lunchroom and stairwells were clean. They checked on whether teachers were using the assigned textbooks, how unruly the students were, how the staff dealt with bad behavior, and who was in the building besides teachers and students. Above all, they wanted evidence that the school had a firm grasp of the state standards that spelled out exactly which skills students needed to master in each grade.

But since the inspectors focused so much on the school's

physical appearance, these spot checks were like taking someone's temperature to determine whether a bone was broken. The
evidence they were looking for could be faked, and many failing
schools had become expert fakers. It was easy enough for a
school to post cheerful, perfect work samples—doctored by
teachers—and trick the inspectors into thinking it was on the
right course.

Usually, though, schools had some advance notice before a
state visit. Now, Buchanan was giving Donna a rapid rundown
of how her classroom should look, and how Donna should act if
the monitors crossed her threshold. The number-one rule, she
said, was to update the schedule on the blackboard so that it pre-
cisely reflected Donna's plans for the afternoon. Although
Buchanan and others had stressed the importance of keeping
the schedule current, Donna rarely bothered to rearrange it
every day, since she knew it by heart.

Besides, Donna was nowhere near adept at keeping a strict
schedule—some lessons still went far longer than forty-five
minutes, or ended far sooner if behavior was bad. Donna also
made last-second changes sometimes, delaying math until the
end of the day if the students were especially hyper after lunch,
or skipping science to do an extra-long social studies unit. (Such
deviations were frowned on at P.S. 92, whose curriculum and
schedule were intentionally rigid because giving teachers more
leeway had failed students in the past.)

At lunchtime, Buchanan returned with scissors, tape, and
construction paper. She and Robertson had decided the walls in
Donna's classroom needed to be more "print-rich"—with examples of student work that explicitly met state standards.
Buchanan had scolded Donna repeatedly about putting up more
"standards-driven" work, to avoid complaints from visiting offi-

cials like the ones expected any minute. Here was the perfect reason to put Donna's feet to the fire. She helped Donna line the walls with the construction paper, then post some writing and math exercises. Each had to be graded with a number from one (not meeting standards at all) to four (exceeding standards), with a line or two from Donna explaining why.

As they snipped and taped feverishly, Brenda Robertson's brisk voice came over the public address system. "It is extremely important to keep students in the classrooms and out of the halls," she warned. "Teaching and learning should be occurring in every classroom. Please check for any errors on your boards. It is very important to put our best foot forward."

Donna, who had at first treated the interruption as a petty annoyance, was starting to sweat. According to her schedule, she was supposed to teach math from 12:50 to 1:35, around the time that the visitors were expected. But she felt that she had not spent enough time preparing, and math was by far her weakest, most neglected subject. She could not stand the thought of the inspectors observing her on such shaky ground, and she said so, but Buchanan was adamant.

"You can't deviate from the schedule on your board," she said. "If they ask you anything, Ms. Moffett, be honest. Don't lie, that's all. Be honest. They don't expect you to have the answers to everything."

A little before 1:00 p.m., two white cars pulled up just below Donna's window and the state monitors emerged. As Donna started the dreaded math lesson (*L.O.: Students will be able to perform subtraction*), she entreated the students to be good and promised them apple juice as a reward. Buchanan parked herself in the back, supervising and waiting for a knock at the door. But when the math lesson ended—on time, for once—the monitors still had not made it to Donna's classroom. Donna actually felt disappointed, since the lesson had gone pretty well. Buchanan even praised her afterward, noting that the students had been "actively engaged" and had understood the lesson.

Donna moved on to one of her twice-weekly science lessons, having the students examine bean sprouts they had planted in paper cups the previous week and write some observations. Then she doled out the promised apple juice and dismissed them, the dreaded knock having never come. Her heart was still thumping faster than usual and her stomach, having missed lunch, was gurgling rebelliously.

Buchanan told Donna that the frantic preparation had been a good experience, anyway. "You know there are certain things I've been asking you to do and keep up with," she said. "Today should really impress on you the importance of taking my suggestions and ideas."

After school on Tuesdays, Wednesdays, and Thursdays, the teachers at P.S. 92 spent forty minutes working on reading and writing with small groups of students in the third through fifth grades. This was part of the special agreement under which teachers at P.S. 92 and a few dozen other schools had agreed to work forty extra minutes, four days a week, in exchange for a 15 percent raise—an experiment in the longer school day that Rudy Giuliani had been pushing for.

Donna had been assigned a group of third-graders, and on the day of the inspection, as usual, they plopped down in a circle on the floor at 2:30. They were reading from a biography of Ida B. Wells, the black newspaper editor who had led a highly public crusade against lynching in the late 1800s. The book was on reading lists throughout the school system, which thought it important to illuminate the scorching realities of racism.

The group had held several passionate discussions about lynching the week before. One student, a boy named Lucas, had volunteered that in fact, his grandfather had been lynched. The children were taking turns reading passages when Brenda Robertson ushered in three state monitors, two men and a woman with calm, friendly looks. They stood off to the side while the reading continued, and Donna, clearly nervous, interjected comments, speaking more quickly than usual.

She launched into a discussion of lynching, which the third-graders had spoken about so poignantly over the last few days. She turned to Lucas, asking a tad too brightly, "What did you tell me the other day about your grandfather? What did you say happened to him?" It was not as if Donna had forgotten; the students knew that, as she was using the tone she reserved for going back over information already learned or discussed. But Lucas, usually a motor mouth, was uncomfortable and shy before the visitors. He offered no response.

"Lucas," Donna said, "I think you said that your grandfather had been lynched. You told me that, didn't you?" The boy nodded silently. "You really should write something about that, Lucas."

They continued reading aloud, but Donna figured it was best to stop and ask questions, since the state learning standards expected students to respond thoughtfully to subject matter. "Can you remember what it means to be lynched?" she said. "Can you describe what it means?"

Tiffany, one of her favorites, offered a matter-of-fact definition. The monitors, all of whom were white, were smiling politely and taking notes, but it was impossible to know what they were thinking.

Was she talking too lightly about one of the most atrocious chapters in the nation's history? Donna certainly did not mean to be insensitive, and if the monitors construed her lesson as such, they did not show it as they impassively filed out. Still, moments like these made uncomfortably stark the cultural gulf separating Donna from her students, which she as yet had little clue how to cross. Not only that, but it showed Donna's intense discomfort with the close supervision that many school systems layer on, a reaction that was hardly unique to her. Coming from the corporate world, she was not used to visitors judging her job performance at close range. And like a stage actress in her first show, she was cowed by the thought of bad reviews, knowing as she did that they could threaten her future, or her school's, with the stroke of a pen. Later, hopefully, such visits would not unnerve her nearly as much, for they would continue throughout her teaching days.

.   .   .

The report cards that Donna sent out in March made it easy to rate her students. They laid out every expectation in tidy phrases like "listens carefully" and "is aware of current events." All she had to do was choose from five grades—excellent, good, satisfactory, needs improvement, or unsatisfactory—and check the right box.

Measuring her own progress was not so simple. Though her summer instructors had recommended visiting veterans' classrooms often during the first year to get a sense of what she should be doing, Donna had managed to do so only a few times. Diana Rahmaan allowed such observations only during prep periods, when the visiting teacher's own class would be covered. But Donna found she needed her once-daily prep period for catching up.

Principals reviewed the performance of their teachers annually in New York, based on occasional observations during the year, but as in most school districts, they had only two options: satisfactory and unsatisfactory. The latter was the first step toward firing a teacher, but the union made it difficult for principals to give "U" ratings by requiring copious documentation and a lengthy appeals process. The ratings said nothing, anyway; teachers' unions had designed them decades earlier to be vague.

Dakota Reyes, the instructional specialist from the Chancellor's District who had dropped by 218 in the fall, had not visited in months because she had so many other responsibilities. Nina Wasserman, the mentor from Brooklyn College around whom Donna relaxed because she was not an official boss, came only once every six weeks. The only advice that Donna got regularly these days was from Marie Buchanan, whose presence made Donna anxious because, after all, she was an emissary of Donna's employer.

Some teachers wryly called Buchanan "the enforcer," because she policed their classrooms and the hallway bulletin boards. Much of Buchanan's advice to Donna dealt with the look and layout of Room 218. She was constantly reproaching Donna for the appearance of something or other, and though her tone was less strident than Brenda Robertson's, it still made Donna bristle.

Buchanan considered Donna a lucky newcomer, and did not let her forget it.

"Back when I was a new teacher, they basically gave you your class and it was on you to make sure you learned the curriculum," she said, brows raised. Buchanan thought that Donna, in contrast, had a whole team of people keeping tabs on her. Only the teaching fellows had mentors watching over them, and Donna had two: Buchanan and Nina Wasserman.

To many in the system, the Teaching Fellows program still

smacked of elitism, even though the chancellor had toned down his public praise of the fellows since fall. The damage had been done early on—he had made it clear that the fellows were his pets, implying they possessed talents that the rank-and-file lacked. Once, a colleague had dryly referred to the teaching fellows as "the Harvard bunch" in Donna's presence. It made Donna want to laugh, since she had graduated from Bronx schools and the solidly working-class City University—as a night student in her forties, at that.

True, Donna had been drawn to the fellows program partly because it was billed as a high-status group of reformers. But Baruch was about as far from Harvard as you could get, and Donna, the daughter of a secretary from Throgs Neck, did not consider herself Ivy League material.

.   .   .

In the beginning, Donna had been respectful toward Buchanan and eager for her advice. Buchanan was chatty and good-humored, and when she had chided Donna, it had been gentle. But as fall turned to winter and Donna began to harden up, she decided that Buchanan criticized far too often, and that she tended to focus on problems that seemed trivial, like the placement of posters on the walls or how often Donna let the students sharpen their pencils.

"She's like a baby learning to walk," Buchanan said of Donna after spending time in her classroom one day. "Right now she's crawling. Someday soon, she'll take tiny little steps."

Buchanan meant well, but she was dealing with a forty-six-year-old, not a twenty-two-year-old who had never experienced the world. Donna was annoyed to be compared with an infant.

She was proud of the life experience she brought to the job, the way she had set up her classroom, and especially her playful, loving rapport with her students. As Buchanan extolled the virtues of strict rules and structure, a line from the essay Donna had written for her Teaching Fellows application rang in her head: "My objective is to convey to children in their formative years the *sheer pleasure* in learning."

The way that Buchanan wanted her to run her classroom was not pleasurable—not for Donna *or* the students. But unlike many of the teaching fellows, Buchanan didn't stop to question orders from above—almost nobody who had worked in the system a long time did, or they would likely have quit or been forced out. In such a top-down, hierarchical system, people got used to being followers and rule-abiders. This was the culture that Harold Levy was hoping the teaching fellows would eventually change, but for now, there were far too few fellows to make a dent.

.   .   .

On her last visit to Room 218, Nina Wasserman had brought a stack of storybooks about clouds. April was approaching, with its inevitable showers, and clouds seemed an ideal subject. For homework, the students could write about rain and sunshine, trees and flowers.

One balmy week in late March, Donna had planned several afternoon literacy lessons around the cloud stories. But Buchanan stopped by 218 one morning with her own game plan. She wanted to watch Donna teach a lesson with a set of textbooks that had been collecting dust on a shelf under the blackboard. No ifs, ands, or buts.

These were the texts that Donna was supposed to use for

every afternoon reading lesson. But in fact, she had largely ignored them. After the rigors of Success for All in the morning and another packaged program, Math Trailblazers, in the early afternoon, the last thing she needed was another teacher's guide choreographing her every move. Donna preferred to read stories that she picked out at this time of day, and to have the children write about topics of her choosing. She had good taste, and surely Nina did, too.

Lately, though, Buchanan had been noticing Donna's neglect of the textbooks. She was fixed on getting them off their shelf. After all, her head would be the first to roll if some Board of Ed official with a clipboard walked in one afternoon and found Donna going off on some unsanctioned tangent. That was why Buchanan had rushed to help Donna get her classroom up to regulation on the day the state inspectors visited. That was one of the most poisonous aspects of a huge system that trusted its school-level employees so little that it operated by inflexible fiat.

"Our reading series is Signatures, and you can't get around it!" Buchanan had said the previous afternoon, when she had walked in to find Donna talking up clouds. "The morning is Success for All, the afternoon is Signatures. A P.S. 92 day is a very structured day."

She would be back, she said, to watch a Signatures lesson the following afternoon.

Donna had not prepared for the lesson that night, hoping Buchanan would not follow through. She thought back to August, when Diana Rahmaan had spotted the Baruch literature prize on her résumé and said Donna's students would benefit from her talents. Now, Buchanan was accusing her of *hurting* the kids by following her own literary instincts.

In truth, Donna could not judge the Signature textbooks well. She had barely looked at them. It was one small piece of the school day, this afternoon reading period, and she wanted to make it *her* piece. It was her best chance—more or less her only chance—to put her own stamp on things.

.   .   .

In moments of composure, Donna believed that Buchanan was helping her become a better teacher—at least, a better P.S. 92 teacher. But was that what she wanted to be? Donna, who had been so devoted to the idea of teaching in a struggling school at the outset, was no longer sure it was a good match for her personality and values. She had envisioned a job in which inventiveness and serendipity could reign, when in fact, the intense pressure to improve test scores made creativity and risk-taking as forbidden as corporal punishment.

Donna was grateful for some of the things Buchanan had taught her, and knew it was selfish to crave the tender nurturing she gave her students. She just wanted to feel respected—even a small hint of respect would make her feel so much better. But she was still waiting.

.   .   .

After lunch that day, Buchanan planted herself in the back of the classroom, arms crossed. Donna handed out the dusty Signatures textbooks and started to pass around the workbooks that went with them.

But Buchanan stopped her. "Don't give them that," she snapped.

The textbook was divided into themes, and the first was called "Pets Are Special Animals."

"Pets help children learn responsibility and provide ways for sharing love," the teacher's guide in Donna's hand read. "The selections in this theme enable readers to discover how having a pet can be a meaningful experience."

Donna had spent only about five minutes skimming the guide over her lunch break. She had decided to approach the lesson as if it were Success for All.

"Let's open to page 11: 'Pets Are Special Animals,'" Donna told the class. "Point to the word *Meet*." She read the first line, then had the students repeat it.

They proceeded that way, with Donna reading about pets and the students repeating after her, sentence after sentence. They were parroting what she said so unthinkingly that when she said "Very good" at the end of a passage, most echoed "Very good" in her exact cadence. It was hard to tell whether they were absorbing anything.

Buchanan was exasperated. Good teachers give their students an introduction to the subject matter before jumping into the text, she thought. They go over relevant vocabulary and get their students excited about the topic by asking them questions for at least five minutes.

A page or two into the story, when she got her bearings, Donna had stopped to ask the children if they had dogs or cats at home. She was on the right track, Buchanan thought. But if Donna had been prepared, she would have asked that question before starting.

"You just can't wing a reading lesson," Buchanan muttered, wondering why Donna had not prepared the night before.

It would have taken an hour, at the most, because the teacher's guide was fairly explicit. In Buchanan's mind, that was the beauty of the structured lessons that P.S. 92 favored, especially for new teachers. All you had to do was spend a little time looking over the script.

After the preface about pets came a story by Ezra Jack Keats—real children's literature, Donna had to admit—called *Dreams*. "In this amusing story, children will learn how a boy's tiny paper mouse manages to scare away a very real and threatening dog," it said.

The lesson had been going on for twenty-five minutes, and the students had stopped following the text with their fingers. A few were drifting. So Donna began reading more dramatically, lowering her voice to imitate a boy and cackling for a pet parrot's lines. The class brightened.

But Buchanan shook her head and sighed. Donna was making a game of it with silly voices, and distracting the children from the story line. Buchanan thought Donna made a game of lessons far too often. She would start out following the program, but quickly slip into experimentation, doing things her own way.

Donna moved on to a short biography of Ezra Jack Keats, and smiled when she read that as a child, he had scribbled on a table in his house. "Ah-*ha*!" she said. "Just like some students in here!" Giggles ensued.

"Um, you don't have to say that," Buchanan called from the back of the room.

Though Donna did not do it today, Buchanan had seen her stop in the middle of a lesson and announce it was time to "shake the sillies out." The students would get out of their seats, waggle their torsos, and wave their arms as they joined Donna in a Raffi song:

> I've got to shake, shake, shake my sillies out,
> Shake, shake, shake my sillies out.
> Shake, shake, shake my sillies out . . .

A bad idea, Buchanan thought: taking little kids' minds off the lesson, in the middle of it, when their attention spans were nonexistent to begin with. A few would be able to pick back up after jumping around, but many, like Cindy and Curtis, would not. What she did not acknowledge was that Donna had a gift for making lessons fun, and that the pleasure the students got from her jokes, songs, and dances often made them more, not less, engaged. Maybe the least intelligent, most apathetic teachers should be kept on the tightest leash possible, but Donna was not in that category, and as Nina Wasserman firmly believed, her charisma was a great asset.

Donna scanned the teacher's guide, saw that she was now supposed to ask the students which characters in the Keats story seemed real. Using a Success for All strategy, she told them to "buddy buzz," working in pairs to come up with answers. Most produced good answers; it was a small victory. Buchanan approved because P.S. 92 teachers were supposed to incorporate Success for All techniques into all their lessons.

Flipping the page of her teacher's guide, Donna saw that the next and last step in the lesson was an art project. The class was supposed to make paper animals like the ones in the book. But the directions were fairly elaborate: Each student would need a piece of construction paper, scissors, crayons, and glue. Reading the instructions out loud like a recipe, Donna scurried to her supply cabinet for a stack of paper.

But there was Buchanan, holding up her hand and pointing to her watch. Math was to begin in twelve minutes. For once, Donna would have to start on time.

"You're not going to have time to complete that," Buchanan announced.

Donna shoved the paper back into the cabinet and shut it with more force than necessary, lips pursed. Buchanan approached.

"You have to prepare for these lessons, and you have to closely follow your teacher's guide," she said quietly. "Tomorrow we are going to do this again, and you're not going to wing it."

Buchanan suggested that the students spend the last few minutes of the lesson writing about the Ezra Jack Keats story. But Donna rebelled, asking each student to read a sentence of the story out loud instead. Jamilla did well, reading two sentences and not wanting to stop. But Briella stumbled, and Donna had to read her sentence for her. Discouraged, she returned to having the whole class repeat after her.

By now, Trevor was squirming and Stefanie's head was on her desk, her face blank. Buchanan announced that it was time to wind down, and Donna flashed her a fierce look.

"When you say wind down, do you mean stop?" she asked curtly, then smacked her teacher's guide shut.

"Boys and girls, put away your Signature books in your desks and take out your math books."

Donna had prepared for the math lesson (*L.O.: Students will review the concept of area*), and did a good job with it. But when Buchanan finally left, she ended the lesson early and had the students start copying down their homework assignment. Her back ached and she felt like sobbing. The anger that had enveloped her earlier had given way to a sense of utter defeat. Why would Buchanan reprimand her in front of the children? Donna wondered whether the administration was trying to drive her out.

By the time everyone copied down the homework assignment, only twenty minutes remained for science. Donna had the students glue cut-out fruits and vegetables to construction paper as she tried to keep her emotions in check. Then, as everyone packed up for the night, one last challenge confronted her. Cindy started crying because she could not find her notebook.

When Donna spoke more sharply than usual, telling her that they would search for it in the morning, Cindy crumpled to the floor and wailed. The patience that Donna had meted out during Buchanan's visit was gone. Her day had been ruined, and this child was dealing a final blow that felt insufferable.

"Okay, I'm calling security," she barked, making Cindy cry harder.

It was the wrong tone, and the wrong thing to say to a six-year-old. Donna knew it. But every ounce of compassion had drained from her that afternoon. She left Cindy on the floor and was lining up the others for dismissal when Buchanan strolled back in and eyed the distraught child with surprise.

As Donna walked the class downstairs, Buchanan knelt to look Cindy in the eye. In her face was just the kind of motherly concern that Cindy needed to see. It made sense that this girl who was always looking to acquire things and squirrel them away, from extra snacks to other children's property, would hate to lose one of her own possessions. Buchanan understood that, though at the moment, Donna was too frazzled to.

"I would feel bad, too, if I lost my notebook," Buchanan said, stroking Cindy's glossy black hair and dabbing at her tears. "How would you like to go downstairs with me and get a new notebook?"

Cindy kept moaning, but her tears stopped and she looked appreciative. She was calm as Buchanan took her hand and walked her out of the room.

.   .   .

That night, Donna called Nina to describe the awkward Signatures lesson and vent. But Nina pleaded with her to be humble, and to gracefully accept whatever criticism Buchanan doled out.

"That is part of being a superior teacher," she said, trying to calm Donna down. A superior teacher could face all supervisors with equanimity, accepting their advice and making them feel respected without—and this was the key, in Nina's view—abandoning her own instincts.

It would help immeasurably, Nina said, to visit some more progressive, successful schools that allowed teachers more leeway in their own lesson-planning. Then Donna could bring some of the more creative practices she observed back to her own classroom and meld them with the P.S. 92 curriculum.

But until Donna knew what those time-tested practices were, Nina said, she should follow the P.S. 92 program.

"The trick is to take what Buchanan is telling you and use only what you absolutely need, and still persist with what you know these children need and what you do so well."

Donna had returned to P.S. 92 the next day determined to heed Nina's advice. But later in the week, she again felt close to a meltdown. She was trying to do the right thing: another lesson with the Signatures books. But Buchanan had come to observe yet again, and she was interrupting and reproaching even more than the last time. For this lesson she stayed at Donna's side, looking over her shoulder.

It felt suffocating, and Donna snapped. She wheeled around to face Buchanan suddenly, eyes blazing.

"Why don't I leave the room and *you* finish the lesson?" she said, and headed for the door. But as she reached for the knob, Buchanan's voice halted her.

"Ms. Moffett. *No.*"

Buchanan strode to the door and blocked it, staring Donna

down. It was the tensest moment Donna had experienced since her face-off with Brenda Robertson in October.

"Ms. Moffett, I'm not letting you leave this room," Buchanan said. "You go back there and you finish that lesson."

"You're on my back constantly," Donna shot back. "I can't take this anymore."

But as the two women glared at each other, Nina's advice came flooding back, and Donna forced herself to back down. There were twenty children watching and waiting. She was not going anywhere.

She was surprised at the calm that enveloped her as she finished the lesson. Afterwards, she apologized to Buchanan.

"I've never done anything like this," Donna said. "I hope you'll forgive me. It was totally unprofessional."

.   .   .

Over the next month, as tulips bloomed in a little garden next to P.S. 92 and the Easter break approached, Donna and Buchanan came to an understanding. They talked after their showdown in the doorway of 218, and Buchanan said that she could not let Donna's spite for the P.S. 92 curriculum jeopardize her own career. Donna said that she understood, but that her ego had been badly bruised.

"I feel like not only can you not tolerate me, but you really wish I wasn't here at all," Donna said, chastened but still smarting.

"If I didn't want you here you'd know it," Buchanan replied, "because I'd ignore you. I have plenty of other things to do."

"I'm an old dog," Donna said, "and I'm trying to learn all these new tricks."

In the weeks that followed, when Buchanan visited 218 she either stayed quiet or helped out in a way that Donna found constructive, not insulting. She did believe Donna was making
progress, mostly because Donna was taking more of her advice.
She was using the Signature books. And she was arranging her
bulletin boards more to Buchanan's liking, putting up only the
best examples of "standards-driven" work instead of cramming
them with work by every student.

Though she had not told Donna, Buchanan was even starting
to think that she would be an excellent teacher some day. Though
Donna would not have guessed it, Buchanan admired how
much enthusiasm and energy she brought to the job, and believed it would take her far. She just wished that Donna would
feel more relaxed about learning to teach, let the scripted curriculum do the work for her and not try to add her own volatile
mix of ingredients.

"Rome wasn't built in a day, Ms. Moffett," Buchanan was
fond of saying. She, like Diana Rahmaan, believed it took five
years for a teacher to learn her craft—five years of soaking up
advice and following directions, not conducting your own experiments. Donna Moffett had a good shot, Buchanan thought, but
she would have to get over her superiority complex first.

Since four out of five new teachers left within five years—
often because of the same frustrations that were plaguing Donna
that spring—she would also have to beat tremendous odds.

.   .   .

Her latest conflict past, Donna felt hopeful as the weather got
warmer and the streetscapes of Flatbush became a little gentler,
a little easier on the eyes. Spring was finally energizing Donna,

and she wanted to inject some of that energy into her students during their lunch hour, when they complained that there was nothing to do in the schoolyard. One day, she delighted them by coming out to play as they huddled and trudged around the scabrous asphalt.

As other children and the lunch aides looked on incredulously, Donna led her class in rounds of jumping jacks and stretches. It was the closest thing to gym class they would have that year. Later in the week, she brought in rubber balls, jacks, and other toys to keep them from chasing and teasing each other—the usual rituals—during recess. It felt much more productive to play jacks with Nicole and Angelique than to sit on a nearby bench and stew.

They were discussing the landmarks of their neighborhood in social studies, and one afternoon, Donna and Ruth Baptiste walked the class to the local library, stopping along the way for coconut buns at a Caribbean bakery. Melissa's mother had surprised her by writing, "Keep up the good work!" on the field trip permission slip.

Donna was planning a series of class outings around the neighborhood: to the Brooklyn College theater, the Brooklyn Botanical Garden, and the Prospect Park Zoo. She loved getting the students out of P.S. 92 and into the community, which they always regarded with as much wonder as if it were their first time exploring it. Colleen Dewgard, the young guidance counselor who had been working with Melissa, now took Tasha, Manette, and Melissa out of the classroom together a few times a week, just to talk. About half the students were at least attempting their homework assignments, an improvement from the winter.

Donna was more comfortable with Success for All now— when she deviated from the script, it was usually in a way that helped the children understand. Sounding out the letter *I*, for example, Donna said, "Like *Cindy*. Like *Nicole*. Like *Melissa*." Sometimes, when their attention was wavering and Buchanan was not hovering, Donna affected a French or Spanish accent as she read the script, and they usually snapped back. "Vive la difference!" she trilled one morning as they studied the difference between a lower-case and upper-case *K*.

In late April, Donna decided to pay homage to her past life and celebrate Secretaries Day. The class had been talking and writing about careers all month, and the students had written beautiful essays about what they wanted to be when they grew up. The standouts belonged to Marsha, who wanted to be a police officer, and Trevor, who wanted to be God. Now, Donna wanted to tell them about her old job, partly because she knew several of their mothers and grandmothers were secretaries.

Donna had brought in bouquets for the students to present to the four secretaries in the main office, and they marched excitedly downstairs that morning after lunch. But Buchanan spotted the class in the hallway and, to Donna's surprise, ordered them back to 218. The third- and fifth-graders were taking standardized tests on the upper floors that morning, and she did not want the risk of a noisy hallway.

Donna felt humiliated, and the day she had planned so cheerfully went downhill. During the afternoon literacy lesson (*L.O.: Students will describe what secretaries do at work*), she was less tolerant than usual of misdemeanors, yelling at Briella for playing with a Band-Aid on her finger and sending Monique to the back of the room for not opening her notebook promptly. She also exiled Trevor and Cindy to a kindergarten classroom on the first floor, a new punishment that she had been given permission to use on students who interrupted lessons.

When Donna tried to take the students out for a bathroom break just before lunch, Buchanan once again stopped them in their tracks. Testing was still underway.

After lunch, Donna's students were even more out of sorts than she was. Jamilla was crying, and Shakeela, Melissa, and Tasha were asking if their parents could pick them up early because they felt sick. Nicole began to cry, too, saying her stomach hurt. The afternoon literacy lesson, with the Signatures books, was supposed to be getting underway. Donna's lesson plans said that the class would read a story from the books, then discuss characters, plot, setting, and conflict. But by now, Nicole and Jamilla were crying so hard about their supposed aches and pains that Donna told them to go lie down on the reading mat. Tasha was joining in the sob fest, and Cindy was trying hard to bring tears to her own eyes, screwing up her face and moaning. Curtis was acting like a maniac: playing an invisible piano Jerry Lee Lewis–style, rolling his eyes back in his head and snorting. Donna decided it was an appropriate time to improvise.

"Put your heads on your desks and close your eyes," she said, popping a classical music cassette into an old tape player she had brought in.

The longer she taught little kids, the more Donna saw that sometimes, everything goes kablooey for no apparent reason and the teacher has no choice but to improvise. The trick was to have a box full of tools, so to speak, to address all kinds of problems and behaviors. Donna did not yet have a full box, but the strategy she spontaneously devised was a sound one.

As they rested, Donna wrote on the board: *L.O.: Students will discuss and write about how to stay well.* She passed out construction paper and wrote more instructions on the board: Draw you

eating foods that are good for you. Draw you doing exercise.
Draw you sleeping. When she roused them five minutes later,
she chided, "Ms. Moffett's stomach hurt yesterday, but I kept
teaching all day."

It might not be a Signatures lesson, but Donna had managed
to engage the students and stop their crying—and she had done
so with a more advanced technique than simply taking them to
the playground, her last resort in the fall. Tasha, with Donna's
help, wrote, "I like broccoli." Angelique drew seven foods in intricate detail and labeled them, spelling perfectly. Monique drew
a picture of herself and a dog and wrote above it, "I like health
food." Nicole sounded out the words *banana* and *milk* and wrote
them imperfectly.

"This has been a very difficult day," Donna sighed as the children got their coats at dismissal. The only bit of comforting
realism that a teacher movie had offered was a scene from *Blackboard Jungle* that occurred to her on days like this, when the new
teacher, so tortured that he's ready to quit, seeks advice from his
wise old college professor. "Is there no way to get to those kids?"
the teacher asks. "Is there no way to make them understand?"

"You'll find a way," the professor responds.

To Donna, that simple answer suggested there was no formula—no single path that she had somehow failed to follow.
Every teacher had to keep searching for the right way, the way to
make it work for her and the particular set of students she had
been dealt. When this year was over and she had a new class, she
might have to find a whole new way.

She was keenly aware that it was only April, and that she still
had an enormous amount of material to cover. One flight up, the
third-graders were finishing the tests that would determine
whether or not they were promoted to the next grade, and the

results would factor into P.S. 92's own tenuous fate. Donna's students would be taking the same exams in two short years. It was hard to imagine them being ready, but at least she was taking baby steps toward getting them there, finding a way.

CHAPTER EIGHT

L.O.: Students will write about their mothers.

Mother's Day was just around the corner, and Donna wanted her students to describe their moms in essays for her May bulletin board, which was supposed to be up by the end of the day. "Who? What?" she wrote on the blackboard as a guide, then asked them to write a few sentences. "Talk to your writing partner," she instructed, pacing in front of the board. "Plan what you're going to say. When do you see your mommy? When do you have fun with her? What is your mommy's name?"

Shane and Briella could not answer this last question, and asked hopefully whether they could skip the assignment. Trevor said he had nothing to write about because his mother did nothing interesting. "She lay on the couch and watch TV," he said.

Though only the second week of May, it was 88 degrees in the classroom, according to a thermometer Donna had brought in for a weather-related science lesson. The heat was threatening her powers of concentration, not to mention the children's. A gleaming new air conditioner had loomed over one of the classroom windows since September, but Donna was not allowed to switch it on. To save money, the Board of Ed permitted air conditioning only in summer school, which began after the Fourth of July.

Diana Rahmaan's weekly memo to her staff had alluded to the sultry weather, warning that it was no excuse for slacking off. This was high testing season, with third- and fifth-graders taking the city reading exam the following week and fourth-graders preparing for the state math exam at the end of the month.

"As the weather warms up and the end of the year approaches, we can expect that our students will become a bit anxious," Rahmaan had written, using what seemed a euphemism for "out of control."

"Therefore," Rahmaan had continued, "I am reminding all of us that we must be very diligent in the preparation of full-period activities and do not allow for 'down time,' which is a major cause of poor tone. Our children don't need a rest from academics—they must continue to be pressed to strive for the best. Down time is not a reward, it is a theft of instruction."

A steamy classroom was more likely to cause poor tone than a few minutes of down time, Donna thought dryly. She had never done well in the heat and had not needed to until now, since law firms never lacked for air conditioning. Although September had also sizzled in Room 218, Donna had been so consumed by her new responsibilities that she had barely noticed the discomfort.

Rahmaan had told the first-grade teachers to focus on writing as the school year wound down, making sure their students used proper punctuation and could distinguish questions from declarative sentences. So Donna did not feel as bad as usual when the afternoon literacy period went almost an hour late that day, swallowing math. The students enjoyed the assignment, writing funny, lively, touching sentences about their mothers. Donna's excitement was palpable as she leaned over their desks, massaged their shoulders, and said, "Now we're cooking!" and "All right, 218!" She was feeling confident and was in her element, having the students write about someone they loved. She almost forgot about the heat.

Though Diana Rahmaan had told her staff to focus on writing for the last eight weeks of school, math was weighing heavily on their minds by early June. The talk in the weekly faculty meetings had already turned to September, and foremost among Rahmaan's goals was improving scores on the high-stakes math exams.

It was a sharp philosophical change for P.S. 92, because for all the years that the school had been on the "failing" list, the most pressing priority had been getting children to read and write. It was, in fact, a system-wide belief that reading skills were by far the most crucial to impart, and that the reading curriculum at every troubled school deserved the most time, thought, and energy. Rudy Crew had ardently pushed this approach when he became chancellor in 1995, proclaiming that all 1.1 million city schoolchildren should be reading by the end of third grade. Crew had come nowhere near reaching that lofty goal by the time he was ousted in 1999, but his efforts had reaped some fruit: Reading scores climbed modestly during his tenure, especially in the early grades, where he had invested the most money and attention. It was Crew who insisted that Chancellor's District schools have no more than twenty children in kindergarten through third-grade classrooms, for example, and that all students in those grades have their reading and writing skills formally assessed every fall and spring to track progress.

P.S. 92 was among the schools where the approach was paying off: Only about 16 percent of fourth-graders were reading at or above grade level in 1999, just before Crew ordered the school into the Chancellor's District. Two years later, the number had jumped to 25 percent—still dismal, but markedly better. Diana Rahmaan believed that Success for All was largely responsible, combined with an extraordinary amount of hard work and dedication on the teachers' part. The teachers' union, whose members complained even more about crowded classrooms than about their low pay, credited the small class size that P.S. 92 enjoyed because it was in the Chancellor's District, and the forty extra minutes of instruction a day that it had agreed to.

In math, the news had not been nearly as good. Only 18.6 percent of P.S. 92 students who took standardized math tests in 1999 had passed, and two years later—despite hundreds of thousands of dollars in extra resources and a new schoolwide math program—the number had dropped to 14.8 percent. Clearly math instruction had been neglected, and Donna was as much to blame as anyone. How many afternoons had she impulsively decided to abbreviate a math lesson, or worse, skip it altogether? The neglect had not always been willful. It was just difficult to conduct strong, meaningful lessons in a subject she had always shied away from.

Marie Buchanan kept a close eye on Donna's literacy lessons and gave her more tips than she wanted, lord knows. But there had been much less supervision in math. This weakness was not unusual—poorly prepared math instructors were the norm in New York and other troubled school systems around the country. Education schools spent far more time training elementary school teachers in reading than in math, not only because they considered reading a more urgently important subject, but because professors tended to be more comfortable teaching it. The few college graduates who majored in math could easily get high-paying jobs, so most people teaching middle- and high-school math were not even qualified to do so.

A few years earlier, the Board of Ed had gone so far as to import a few dozen math teachers from Austria because they were well prepared and eager to live in New York City. But they had trouble adjusting to the harsh realities of New York high schools, and besides, immigration laws kept them from staying more than a year or two. With so few options, New York City would remain desperate for good math teachers until the teachers' union allowed higher salaries for people with math expertise, a system that would undermine its ideal of equal treatment for every member.

Donna had begun shying away from math in high school, stopping with trigonometry in the eleventh grade. She so much preferred literature, which sparked her imagination and, in her own dreamy words, nourished her soul. While a few teaching fellows she had met or heard about were engineers or accountants in their past careers, able and eager to take on the challenge of teaching math in failing schools, most seemed like herself: inclined toward literature, and eager to pass their own love of reading and writing on to children who had little or no exposure to its pleasures.

Even if they had been strong math students, the fellows and other teachers were likely to struggle with Math Trailblazers, the program that the Board of Ed had chosen for the Chancellor's District. It took a "constructivist" approach, minimizing the paper-and-pencil arithmetic that Donna and many other teachers remembered from their own school days. Instead of teaching the traditional borrowing and carrying, for example, Math Trailblazers encouraged students to think up their own ways to solve problems, perhaps using blocks, tally marks, or their fingers. The point was for students to understand and be able to explain the methods they used to solve a problem, because the benchmark state math exams in the fourth and eighth grades now required students to write out how they arrived at their answers.

Though not as high profile as the reading wars, a national battle over math instruction had emerged during the 1990s, pitting proponents of the "new math" constructivist approach against those who preferred old-fashioned teaching through memorization and rules. As in the reading debate, conservatives embraced the traditional approach, while progressives countered that it was too boring or daunting for many students. Instead, the progressives said, students should construct their own creative solutions to math problems. The National Council of Teachers of Mathematics, the world's largest organization of math teachers, had published new math standards in 1989 that embraced constructivism, and Math Trailblazers was designed with those standards in mind.

On the surface, it was odd for the Chancellor's District to use a progressive-leaning math program alongside its traditionalist reading program. But the officials who set up the district believed in the constructivist approach, and thought that Math Trailblazers, put out by the Kendall/Hunt Publishing Company, was easier for teachers to learn than many other programs of its ilk. Like Success for All, it was a packaged program that entire schools could use, making it easier to train teachers and providing consistency for students as they moved from grade to grade.

Donna was so far behind on the Math Trailblazers lessons that she had no hope of catching up by the end of June. At a staff meeting early in the month, she had asked whether she needed to reach Unit 20: "Looking Back at First Grade." Rahmaan had not seemed overly concerned, and had told her to go back over some of the lessons she felt shaky on instead of plowing ahead. There were "Cubes and Volume," "Exploring 3-D Shapes," "Fractions and Decimals." So many concepts for first-graders, who in Donna's Catholic school childhood had been assigned only simple addition and subtraction.

To her regret, Donna had not been able to keep up with her fall graduate course on teaching math. Tuesday after Tuesday she'd found that she could not propel herself out of 218 in time for the 6:00 p.m. class.

Nor had Donna possessed any desire to sit through those tedious, three-hour lectures, which were all but irrelevant to her reading-heavy routine in Room 218. She had ultimately withdrawn from the course, to avoid getting an F. Even now, when it was clear she would complete this first grueling year of teaching, Donna was hard on herself for that shortcoming.

Whenever she cut short a math lesson in May and June, she told herself that the following year, she would do penance by learning the Math Trailblazers curriculum backwards and forwards. The new emphasis on math would not play to her strengths, but she was determined—even eager—to come back and work on her weaknesses. That Donna was thinking ahead to September was significant, for dozens of other teaching fellows were looking to June 27 like a finish line—they were not planning to return for a second year.

Like Donna, legions of fellows had fumbled their way through the first year of teaching, enduring abuse from superiors, scattershot or nonexistent on-the-job training, and constant discipline problems in their classrooms. Not all, however, had borne it out to April. About 50 of the 323 fellows who started teaching in September, or 16 percent, had quit the program and abandoned the school system by spring break. Vicki Bernstein had kept a log of their reasons for quitting, most of which were variations on one theme:

"Students threatening him . . . just too overwhelming." "Felt she was not trained properly for an environment of chaos." "Felt unsuited for the experience." "Overwhelmed and uncomfortable yelling at the students every day to get them involved in lessons." "Could not continue working at an administratively inept school." "Did not believe in the school curriculum." "Exhausted and overwhelmed with the constant struggle of misbehavior, profanity, and physical altercations within the classroom."

Most of the fifty dropouts had left between mid-September and late October—the period when Donna had fallen sick, battled with Brenda Robertson, and considered leaving P.S. 92. Clearly the fellows needed far more support than they had gotten during those first, critical months. But it had to come from their colleagues in the schools, and it would require far more than an edict from the chancellor. What was needed was a profound cultural shift and building of trust that would take time. For one thing, the lifers in the school system needed to see that outsiders—from corporate lawyers-turned-chancellors to legal secretaries-turned-teachers—were committed for the long haul, not just briefly acting out a fantasy.

Though less than ideal—especially for the dozens of students who came to school one morning to find their teacher gone—the attrition rate for the fellows was not as bad as nay-sayers had predicted. Still, it was higher than the general rate of 13 percent for first-year teachers in New York City that a State University of New York study had found in 1999. And Harold Levy wondered how many would leave after they got their free master's degree the following spring. The Board of Ed had a lot riding on this investment, and no way of knowing how it would play out.

Levy was seeking 1,500 new fellows for September—nearly

five times as many as had been in the inaugural class. He had met New York State's demand to place only certified teachers in the one hundred worst schools, but there was no telling how many new vacancies would arise in those schools by September. Meanwhile, the clock was ticking toward a much more daunting deadline: Starting in September 2003, the state would not allow *any* uncertified teachers citywide. That meant finding upwards of twenty thousand recruits over the next thirty months who already had certification, or would endure the stress of the fellows program to get it.

The Board of Ed had mounted an international recruitment drive that spring, trolling for experienced teachers in Austria, Germany, Hungary, Italy, Spain, Canada, and several Caribbean countries. It was also casting a far wider net for teaching fellows this year, running newspaper ads not just in New York but Boston, Miami, Philadelphia, Washington, and Puerto Rico. New York hoped to hire as many as eight hundred qualified candidates from overseas to stay in compliance with the new ban on uncertified teachers in failing schools.

But as it would find out, teachers who moved from as far as Jamaica and Budapest would struggle to find affordable housing and adjust to urban American schools. Most would be allowed to stay only three years, on special visas; many would leave even earlier. Levy knew that foreign recruitment was a stopgap measure and not a long-term solution, as he hoped the Teaching Fellows program would be. But he expected to need 8,000 new teachers in September, and without a new teachers' contract offering higher salaries—it would be another year until Levy, Giuliani, and the union came to an agreement—he had to put together a patchwork hiring plan.

Levy was aiming for a more racially diverse applicant pool

this time, so he was running ads in Haitian-Creole, Chinese, and Spanish-language newspapers. Only about 30 percent of the fellows in Donna's group were black and Hispanic, though virtually all of the children they were teaching belonged to those races, since white and Asian children almost unvaryingly attended better schools. Many white fellows had experienced culture clash and racial tensions in their schools, and Levy was hoping that if more fellows were of color, schools and parents in minority neighborhoods would be more accepting of the program.

Levy had hired TBWA\Chiat\Day, the high-powered advertising firm behind Absolut Vodka, Apple Computer, and Levi's, to create catchy new ads for the Teaching Fellows program and the Board of Ed's general recruitment drive. Levy had caught hell from Board of Ed members and the city teachers' union for spending $8 million on the ad campaign, and for turning to one of the flashiest firms on Madison Avenue. Until then, recruitment ads (with the exception of "Sad Girl") had always been designed in-house. But as Levy had made clear with the fellows program, he believed outsiders could bring a fresher, more creative approach than the school system's permanent bureaucracy.

This time, though, he might have overreached. The Chiat\Day team in charge of the ad campaign was brimming with the ironic wit that dominated so many flashy ads aimed at the twenty-something demographic, and Bernstein felt that their tone was totally wrong.

One ad featured the cast of *Welcome Back, Kotter*, the '70s sitcom about a wisecracking high school teacher and his raucous class in Brooklyn. "We need you to be Kotter," it begged. Another alluded to Save the Children, whose ads featured the actress Sally Struthers seeking sponsors for destitute kids in third-world countries. "Are you going to help," the ad asked, "or do we need to call in Sally Struthers?"

Finally, Chiat\Day came up with two ads that Bernstein could live with. One resembled "Sad Girl": "Do you believe all of NYC's students deserve a quality education?" asked the ad, splashed with yearbook-type pictures of cute city kids. "Prove it." The other, written in a child's shaky script, said simply: "Sign up for the most important job in New York City."

Levy and Bernstein knew well that the four weeks of training for Donna's group had been pitifully brief and unorganized. So the second class of fellows would report for duty on June 15 instead of July 31, getting seven weeks of boot camp instead of four. They would spend much of July student-teaching in summer-school classrooms around the city, getting the kind of hands-on preparation that had been achingly absent from Donna's training.

Though summer school was a breeze compared with the regular school year—there were only ten or so students per class, and the day ended at lunchtime—the new fellows would at least have a taste of teaching before getting their own classrooms. Levy also planned to assign some fellows as "co-teachers" in experienced teachers' classrooms for at least the first half of the school year. Such a set-up would have made the transition to teaching much smoother for Donna, as long as she worked well with the experienced teacher whose classroom she was assigned to. It was a great idea, but too expensive.

In the most significant change, not all of the second group of fellows would be sent to New York City's worst schools. With up to 1,500 new fellows, and other certified teachers coming from abroad, there would be more than enough to fill whatever vacancies arose in the one hundred worst schools.

Levy still held fast to his core belief: that the worst schools would never turn around without a critical mass of smart, energetic, risk-taking teachers. Two or three teaching fellows were not enough to make a difference in a failing school, but if the school got ten or fifteen fellows over four years, wouldn't the benefits begin to be palpable? Despite the program's now glaringly obvious flaws, Levy still hewed to the theory that as this first group and subsequent ones learned, they could become "change agents" in their schools, simply because they were impassioned and confident enough to question the status quo.

Yet placing total novices like Donna in the city's most fragile schools had been an act of desperation, spurred by the state's court order. With the crisis past, Levy was curious to see how teaching fellows would do—and if they would be happier—if they started in schools that were less troubled, where they would have more autonomy. That way, Levy thought, they could get their bearings and learn the fundamentals of teaching without struggling under the "check-list" mentality so prevalent in failing schools. Since the fellows were an altruistic bunch, they could probably be persuaded to work in failing schools once they had some experience.

But despite Levy's good intentions, the program was not drawing nearly the number of applicants that he had hoped for. Though the program had received over 2,300 applications in just six weeks the previous spring, only 5,000 had arrived in Bernstein's office from December through March. Bernstein extended the application deadline into April, then May, hoping to reach Levy's target of 1,500 new fellows without compromising the program's selectivity. Ideally, Levy wanted to hire only about one in five applicants, to perpetuate the idea, posted on the Teaching Fellows Web site, that the program accepted only "the brightest minds." But only 7,800 people would apply by the final deadline, and many would lack the requisite 3.0 college grade-point average.

The Board of Ed could only guess why it was not being inundated with applications that spring. For one thing, Levy suspected that the newspaper and television stories about the first class of teaching fellows and their travails had scared people off. One fellow had announced on *Good Morning America* that a student had stolen her wallet, while others had complained to various media outlets about discipline problems and hostile administrators. *The NewsHour with Jim Lehrer* had been airing a yearlong, six-part series about twelve fellows at a school in Bedford-Stuyvesant, Brooklyn, two of whom were so miserable that they quit by January. Another got punched in the face while breaking up a fight between students, and another's class devolved into chaos before the cameras.

Still, the Teaching Fellows Web site was getting about six thousand hits a week, and Bernstein's office was fielding about two hundred calls a day about the program. And the concept was starting to spread around the country, as other urban school districts braced for a teaching shortage. In February, Laura Bush had helped the Washington school system announce a new D.C. Teaching Fellows program modeled after New York's. Similar programs were also in the works for Atlanta, Los Angeles, Denver, Baltimore, Kansas City, Missouri, and Prince George's County, Maryland.

With more retirements looming and few incentives to attract experienced teachers, other districts and entire states were feeling the same immense pressure that New York had the previous year. Massachusetts was offering $20,000 signing bonuses to mid-career professionals who agreed to teach, after the embarrassing revelation that 59 percent of prospective teachers had failed a new basic certification test in 1998. Georgia was rolling out a statewide alternate-route program, Teach for Georgia, that would allow college graduates with at least a 2.5 grade-point average to become teachers after a four-week crash course. Arkansas was eliminating a similar minimum GPA provision in hopes of recruiting more teachers through its existing alternate-route program.

Meanwhile, President Bush had proposed a tenfold increase in federal funding for Troops to Teachers, a program that had recruited military personnel to work in public schools, and a Columbia University program that trained former Peace Corps volunteers to teach was expanding. Alternate-route programs were here to stay, not least because Bush's No Child Left Behind law required a "highly qualified" teacher in every classroom by 2006. Ironically, it said that alternate-route teachers met that definition as long as they passed basic certification tests.

In New York, the fellows program was proving more expensive than Levy had anticipated. Counting summer training, graduate school tuition, and extra pay for teachers serving as mentors to the fellows, the Board of Ed was spending about $25,000 per fellow over two years. That added up to $9 million for Donna's group, and as much as $40 million for the second, larger class. It was a considerable chunk of the school system's $11 billion budget, but the Board of Ed could not afford to hold back.

.   .   .

In the weeks after spring break, Donna's powerlessness to protect her students came home to her in a number of ways. On the first day back, Nicole Peat told Donna that during the week-long vacation, "I cried for you every day." At dismissal, she whimpered, "I don't want to go home," and put her head on her desk. It was painful for Donna to see Nicole, her most affectionate and responsive student, so disconsolate. As the others lined up by the door, Donna took Nicole to the back of the classroom and asked what was wrong.

"My cousin keep beating me up," she said tearfully. "He pick me up and drop me on the ground." She buried her face in Donna's skirt and started crying in earnest.

"My goodness Nicole, I'm so sorry that your cousin is doing that to you," Donna said. "How old is he?"

"He twelve," Nicole answered.

"Does he live with you and your daddy and your brother in your apartment?"

Nicole nodded.

That night, Donna called the Peat residence and reached Nicole's aunt Anna. She told her about Nicole's unhappiness, and repeated what Nicole had said about her cousin, who was Anna's son.

Anna sounded surprised and defensive, Donna reflected afterward. She said that the children in her household were always under adult supervision, and that she had not been aware of any such bullying. Donna hung up feeling exasperated and worried, but not sure what else she could do. Nicole remained out of sorts for the next few weeks, sometimes crying at her desk and often reporting to Donna that other children had teased her.

Around the same time, other students were also enduring frightening experiences. Tasha accused Curtis of touching her bottom in the schoolyard one day, after Patrick and Shane dared him. Donna took the incident seriously, and not only because Tasha was upset. That spring, reports of sexual attacks in city

schools were up 13 percent over the previous year, and were occurring at an average rate of ten per week—more than four
times the national average. Many of the schools reporting the
attacks were huge, like P.S. 92, with only one security guard assigned to them. In one case, two boys, ages ten and eleven, had
been charged with sodomy and sexual abuse of a five-year-old
girl at P.S. 122 in Brooklyn, just blocks from P.S. 92. In another,
two sixth-grade boys were accused of cornering two girls, ages
eleven and twelve, in a stairwell at Community School 66 in the
Bronx. One boy had fondled the breasts and buttocks of the
girls while the other held a door shut, preventing their escape.

In the Bronx attack and several others, school officials had
not notified the police, who found out only after the victimized
children told their families. Harold Levy had a politically
charged crisis on his hands: The incidents became the subject of
lurid newspaper headlines; Rudy Giuliani used them as his latest
excuse to bash the Board of Ed; and parents were understandably furious. Under mounting pressure, Levy had ordered
schools to file formal reports on every case of sex abuse or ha-
rassment. It didn't matter how young the perpetrator was, or
how seemingly minor the offense—with 1,200 schools, such a
sweeping policy was the best chance of making sure no attack
slipped through the cracks, even if it also added to schools' paperwork burdens and blew some incidents out of proportion. All
eighty thousand teachers had been put on notice, so when Tasha
told Donna about the groping, Donna immediately informed
Diana Rahmaan, who followed the new regulations by calling in
all three boys' parents and the police. Patrick, plainly regretful
and frightened, cried during the conference in Rahmaan's office.
His mother could not understand why his schoolyard dare had
provoked such a drastic response.

"I tell him he has to stop hanging around with the wrong people," she told Donna in the hallway afterwards, as Patrick sniffled at her side, "but he says he didn't do anything." Donna was so upset about how the events had played out that she wrote three pages about it in a notebook that night. "What state of affairs have we reached when six-year-olds are considered sexual offenders?" she wondered.

Melissa, meanwhile, was getting mostly zeroes on her spelling tests and slouching through the days. Donna had not heard from her mother since their conference in March, despite several notes to her, and though Melissa seemed to be enjoying her sessions with the counselor, she remained withdrawn in class. One afternoon, Donna had dropped by the main office at 5:00 and found Melissa sitting by the door, still waiting to be picked up. An assistant principal had tried all the phone numbers on the girl's information card, to no avail.

By 6:00, Diana Rahmaan had called the local police precinct to see if something had happened to Melissa's mother. When Rose finally showed up, she said there had simply been a misunderstanding about who would come for Melissa that day. Yet the incident was a fitting symbol of the girl's aloneness.

As if the threats that Donna's students faced at home and in school were not enough, the neighborhood around P.S. 92 held more perils than usual as the few trees on Parkside Avenue bloomed. A man had reportedly been trailing young girls through the neighborhood in a van, and Rahmaan had warned over the public address system, "Never get into cars with strangers." Meanwhile, a poster appeared just inside the front door of P.S. 92, with pictures of several men who had been convicted of sexually abusing or molesting children, had served their sentences, and were being released into the Flatbush community. It wasn't hard to imagine the uproar such a poster would cause in a suburban school. But at P.S. 92, most people seemed to pass it without noticing, as if such hazards were just another fact of life.

. . .

The gloom that had enveloped Nicole did not dissipate in the weeks that followed, despite Donna's efforts. She called on Nicole all the time, squeezed her bony shoulders when she answered correctly, and rewarded her exemplary behavior with lunch in the classroom at least once a week.

And yet Nicole so often seemed bereft, barely interacting with her peers and looking as if she were the only soul for miles around. She complained more often now of slights on the playground and in the lunchroom, saying that other girls had teased her or barred her from sitting with them. Nicole seemed especially hungry for the affections of Angelique, who had recently looked her in the eye and said in her dulcet voice, "I hate you."

From her own school days, Donna knew just how cruel girls who were confident and coveted could be to shy, gawky ones. She had endured her own hell in middle school in the Bronx; one of her clearest memories was of a throng of girls surrounding her in a stairwell, lifting her skirt as a cruel prank. Donna was amazed, however, that her students were acting this catty so far away from puberty.

One morning in early May, Angelique raised her hand urgently and said, "Nicole just hit me on my glasses!" Donna was incredulous. But sure enough, Nicole had allowed herself a tiny burst of rage.

When Donna leaned over the girls and asked, "Can this be

true?" Nicole began crying without tears, horrified by her un-characteristic act of aggression. Her chest was heaving, her cheeks puffing out to arrest the sobs before they escaped her mouth.

Donna led both girls to the front of the room to walk through the Peace Path exercise. Neither Nicole nor Angelique had ever done anything serious enough to warrant the Peace Path, and they were wide-eyed with fear and regret.

"My glasses cost a lot of money," Angelique said weakly as she shuffled forward. "My mother said if I break them, she'll beat me."

Before the girls sat down to write about what happened and how it had made them feel, Donna put an arm around each and hugged them to her. Angelique tried to slip one of her own arms around Nicole for a group hug, but Nicole shrank away, burrow-ing into Donna's skirt like a frightened toddler. Her muffled sobs did not stop until lunchtime, when Donna took her aside as the others lined up at the door.

"How would you like to go to the pizza shop with me while the other students eat their lunch in the cafeteria?" she whis-pered to Nicole. For the first time that morning, a smile lit Nicole's face.

After her classmates filed out, she chose a book from the story corner and read a few pages out loud while Donna sat be-side her. Nicole sounded out the words slowly but for the most part accurately, turning to beam at Donna after each sentence. Donna had rarely had time to sit alone with her students and lis-ten to them read more than a sentence or two. She couldn't help but wonder how much more advanced Nicole might be if she'd had the one-on-one attention she craved.

At the pizzeria, Donna settled into a grimy booth with

Nicole and took out a booklet of pictures, letters, and words. The booklet was part of the Early Childhood Literacy Assessment System, which first-grade teachers throughout New York City used to measure reading and writing skills every fall and spring. Though pop music was blaring and people were wandering in and out of the restaurant, Donna wanted to test Nicole now, while she had her happy and alone.

Nicole was exuberant to have her teacher's full attention, blowing bubbles through her straw and swinging her feet as she studied the words Donna had placed before her. *Get, jump, at, yes, stop. Hand, after, school, don't.* She waded through the word list, recognizing far more this time around than she had in October.

It was a proud moment for Donna: While she had been preoccupied with her problem students over the last few months, something had clicked in Nicole's brain. She had figured out how to blend into words the letters and sounds that Success for All had drilled into her head. Whether Nicole's success was due to the regimentation of her daily lessons, or the confidence that Donna's affection had built in her, or her seriousness of purpose, or some other, intangible factor, Donna would never know. Despite the blunt science of Success for All, this process of learning to read seemed mysterious and, for now, inexplicable.

When she packed the test booklet into her bag and urged Nicole to finish her pizza around 11:00, the girl's sparkle faded. "Why can't we stay and read some more words?" she asked, backing into the corner of their booth.

When they returned to 218 after fetching the other students from the schoolyard, Nicole lingered just outside the door, slurping the rest of her Coke and resuming her forlorn look. Fleetingly as the children took their seats, Donna imagined taking Nicole home with her for a month, or even just a weekend. She wanted a larger hand in Nicole's fate than the one she had been dealt.

.   .   .

One April evening as Donna was leaving her Brooklyn College class, a flyer on a hallway bulletin board caught her eye. For the next few weeks, a community theater group would be performing *Cinderella* in the college auditorium. Donna mulled bringing her class to see the play as one of their last field trips together, but then a more exciting idea seized her. She would bring Nicole, all by herself.

Donna had been longing to do something special for Nicole since their trip to the pizza parlor, when the girl had been so happy to briefly escape with her teacher. Nicole's fall announcement—"I dreamed me and you went on a plane together to somewhere far away"—had been echoing in Donna's mind. Taking the girl to watch a fairy tale—the ultimate escapist fantasy, no less—seemed the perfect plan.

Nicole's quiet father, Marcus Peat, seemed surprised but appreciative when Donna proposed the outing one morning, as he dropped off Nicole in the schoolyard. Peat agreed to let Donna pick up Nicole at his apartment, two blocks from P.S. 92, after lunch on the following Sunday. Donna did not mention the outing to her colleagues, however. She anticipated criticism, and did not want her enthusiasm dampened. The plan did seem a bit subversive—children almost never saw their teachers outside school, and even coincidental meetings were out of the question for Donna and her students, who lived too far apart. If Donna did run into Briella in a Chelsea restaurant, or Trevor at her neighborhood Barnes & Noble, it would feel as extraordinary as spotting a snow leopard in the subway.

Donna had heard other teachers talk about the dangers of getting involved with students and their families. Relations with parents could get tense if your role in their children's lives went beyond that of teacher. Because of that largely unspoken boundary, many of Donna's colleagues did not even give parents their home numbers.

Even within the school itself, the threat of lawsuits always loomed. One teacher was being sued by the mother of a boy whose finger he had accidentally slammed in a classroom door. Donna felt sure that Luis Sanchez, the hyper boy who had been sent to a special school in October, would have jumped out her classroom windows had they not been glued shut. If a teacher took responsibility for a student outside of school, her liability grew exponentially: Nicole could fall off the subway platform or get hit by a car, and Donna would be fully to blame.

.   .   .

Donna looked like a fairy tale character herself as she set out for Brooklyn and *Cinderella* that Sunday afternoon. She wore a long, colorful patchwork dress and flowing black wool wrap, which she needed because the weather had gone from sweltering to unseasonably cool. In her tote bag, she carried treats for Nicole: drawing paper and crayons, and a glow-in-the-dark plastic necklace.

She arrived at Nicole's apartment just on time and rapped on the door, which was thin and covered with peeling paint. The building was a modest wooden row house, like many others that lined Rogers Avenue, the busy thoroughfare around the corner from P.S. 92. When her knock got no response, Donna pushed open the door and saw that it led into a musty, cramped hallway with a narrow staircase that led to another door.

"Hello?" she called.

Hearing nothing but a TV wailing somewhere, she went back outside to check for a rear entrance. There was only a trap door that led to a scary-looking cellar, so Donna returned to the front. Nicole stood on the steps, with an unfamiliar man who blinked in the daylight. He introduced himself as a friend of the family.

It was the first time that Donna had seen her favorite student without the oversized school uniform that made her look so fragile and forlorn. Today, Nicole was dressed in a flowered blue skirt, a white cardigan, and shimmery white sandals. Her smile when she saw Donna was luminous.

They arrived at Brooklyn College early, so Donna took Nicole to a playground on the campus and watched as she scrambled up the slide and had a try on the swings. Nicole was climbing the slide again when a pudgy older boy came up behind her and barked, "Move, asshole!"

Nicole, accustomed to being bullied on the playground, merely stepped aside, but two seconds later Donna was at the slide, grabbing the boy's ankle.

"What kind of language did I hear you use, young man?" she asked. "Is there an adult here with you?"

The boy briefly looked as if he was plotting an escape, but then he pointed to a bored-looking woman on a nearby bench. Donna grabbed Nicole by the hand and marched over to the woman. She'd had many shortcomings that year, but she had never tolerated one child's slight of another.

"Is that your son over there?" she asked hotly. The woman,

startled by the figure in a black cape looming over her, nodded.

"Well, he just used some very troubling language with this little girl and was extremely rude to her," Donna said. "She'd appreciate an apology."

Sheepishly, the woman beckoned her son and forced him to mutter, "Sorry."

Nicole looked deeply contented.

.   .   .

Inside the college auditorium, Nicole raptly followed the story of the maid-turned-princess-for-a-night. She especially loved when the pumpkin turned into a gilded stagecoach, and the rats into white horses. "How they do that?" she asked, and of the wicked stepsisters: "Why they mean to her?"

It was only 4:00 when the play finished, so they strolled the grounds of Brooklyn College for a while, ending up at a big, grassy quadrangle ringed with dignified brick buildings. This was where Donna came for her graduate classes. She had been surprised, when she first saw it, at how much the central campus could pass for a bucolic school in upstate New York or New England. Only the tops of brick row houses, peeking over the far end of the raised quadrangle like an Edward Hopper streetscape, made clear that they were still in central Brooklyn.

Nicole gamboled on the grass, chasing squirrels and running as fast as she could in broad circles. Whatever had made her so unhappy in class over the last month had released its hold. Donna, too, felt buoyant, letting the worries that usually weighted down her Sundays—the next week's lesson plans, for one, which still needed polishing when she got home—fall away. This few hours' respite felt lovely, but Donna was acutely aware that it was fleeting. She kept checking her watch as the daylight faded, as she had promised to get Nicole home by 7:00.

They ate a dinner of curry chicken, plantains, and rice in a shabby storefront restaurant across from P.S. 92—Nicole's choice, over McDonald's—and talked about a field trip to the Prospect Park Zoo that Donna was planning. Donna delivered Nicole home with a sheaf of cheerful pictures she had drawn at the table and the glow-in-the-dark necklace hanging to her waist.

Nicole's aunt Anna answered the door and held out her arms to the exhausted girl. She looked tired herself, Donna noticed, but her manner was pleasant and kind. After thanking Donna, she added: "You have no idea how much this girl talks about Ms. Moffett and everything she learns at school." Anna proudly told Donna that Nicole could read the *Reader's Digests* she subscribed to, and that she had been working with Nicole on her writing.

They parted on what felt like warm terms, and Donna held out new hope that Nicole's sadness was not due to abuse or neglect. Right now, she needed to believe that.

"See you in the morning, Nicole," she said as she turned to go, pulling her wrap tightly against the evening breeze.

"See you tomorrow, Ms. Moffett," came the soft response as the thin door closed and the outing came to a gentle end.

.   .   .

The outing left Donna with a warm, happy feeling, but a few days later, she learned that it had not gone off as perfectly as she'd thought. Nicole's father had approached Donna in the schoolyard one afternoon to say his sister was distraught. After Donna had delivered Nicole home that night, Marcus Peat had told her, Anna had become convinced that Donna was going to report the family to the city's child welfare agency. Was it true, Nicole's soft-spoken father had asked? Did Donna take Nicole out that afternoon just to check up on them and see if she could find any wrongdoing?

Peat revealed that Anna had been upset by Donna's phone call after Easter break, when Donna had asked if her son had hurt Nicole. Donna, shocked, was silent for a moment.

"Why?" she finally managed to blurt out. "Why on earth would your sister think that I was trying to get her in that kind of trouble?"

Donna felt a complicated mix of emotions. On the one hand, she could not believe the Peats would suspect her of trying to take Nicole from them, and was indignant that Anna was suspicious of her generosity. And yet she couldn't deny that she had frequently imagined that Nicole might thrive under different circumstances. Most of all, though, Donna felt a nagging sense of defeat as she stood in the schoolyard with Nicole's father. Perhaps her colleagues had been right: Trying to be part of a student's life outside school could backfire in ways you'd never expect. A teacher could not know the secrets of a family's heart, not in ten short months.

Donna told Nicole's father that she had no intention of reporting Anna, and that she had taken Nicole out that Sunday only to reward her stellar behavior. Peat, who had seemed embarrassed to bring up Anna's fear in the first place, looked satisfied and left the schoolyard smiling his shy, uncertain smile. Donna, however, felt misunderstood, just as she had so many other times that year. She could only hope that she had not made Nicole's life more difficult.

CHAPTER NINE

Despite Diana Rahmaan's admonition against "down time" as the school year drew to a close, P.S. 92 allowed for a few days of fun and relaxation as June set in. The fifth-graders, who would be moving on to middle school in September, were feted with a prom; for Donna's first-graders, the celebrations were more modest. A few weeks before school ended, all of the first-grade classes went together to the Prospect Park Zoo on a day so brilliant that Donna wore her favorite straw hat decorated with huge flowers. She would have liked to make a day of it, but Rahmaan insisted that the students finish their usual ninety minutes of Success for All before departing.

This time, Ruth Baptiste did not come along: The administration had abruptly pulled her from Room 218 in late May, and had reassigned her to work with a disabled child in another class. Donna hated to see her go, but by this time her class was well enough under control. She worried about the children missing Baptiste, but knew they were lucky to have had her for this long.

Manuel's and Angelique's mothers had volunteered to accompany the class, and they brought jumbo bottles of soda and bags of potato chips to complement the bag lunches that the children had brought to eat beside the sea lion pool. The group had just finished lunch when Jamilla, who had been whimpering about feeling sick, threw up on the path to the monkey house. As Donna stroked Jamilla's head and wiped her mouth with a Kleenex while the other students ogled and fidgeted, she might have felt the same dread that had gripped her those first few mornings in the school yard, when she was overwhelmed by the enormity of her new job and the countless things that could go wrong. But instead, Donna felt calm and in control as she divided the class into two groups and asked the two mothers to escort them while she tended to Jamilla. There was only so much a teacher could do in such a situation; nine months into her tenure, Donna understood this and went with the flow. She led Jamilla to the walrus pool and sat beside it in the shade, an arm around the girl and a casual eye on the two groups as they wandered off in the sun.

The days were suddenly passing so quickly—a surprise after all the weeks that had seemed to never end. As Donna's experience of time changed, the question that she had asked herself almost daily for the first half of the year no longer even occurred to her. Almost unconsciously, she had decided to stick with teaching and to stay at P.S. 92 for at least another year.

But while Donna felt more comfortable than ever among her students, her relationship with P.S. 92 continued to be difficult; she still felt isolated from many of her colleagues, though she now admitted that her alienation was at least partly self-imposed. One evening, Nina Wasserman called to say she had arranged for Donna and her students to visit the Brooklyn Children's Museum on June 15. A friend of Nina's worked there, and wanted to give the class a special tour. But when Donna ran the idea by Rahmaan, she again got turned down. The deadline for field trips, as determined by the district office, was June 10—no exceptions, Rahmaan said. As usual, there was no getting around the rules.

Donna reported the conflict back to Nina angrily, but Nina told her to forget about it. "We can do it next year," she said. But these twenty children would not be able to go—at least not with Donna. How aggravating that the top-down style of the Chancellor's District did not even allow for rule-breaking that would *benefit* the kids.

That same week, Donna was in the dog house for not adequately preparing her students for the P.S. 92 dance festival, scheduled for the week before school ended. Every classroom teacher was ordered to choose a dance and practice it to perfection with his or her class. With dark resignation, Donna set about teaching the kids the only dance she knew: the Mexican Hat Dance. Normally she would have reveled in the chance for her students to exercise and express themselves creatively. But she was irked that even year-end festivities would be governed by directive, and that this dictate was eating into her dwindling time with her class.

"I will *not* tolerate this nonsense!" Donna hollered when Tasha uncrossed her arms and Trevor kicked the wrong leg out during brief, sweaty rehearsals in the stuffy gymnasium. Once again, they were bearing the brunt of Donna's anger toward a system she thought unnecessarily rigid and rejecting of ideas that did not come from the top.

That frustration was especially apparent as Donna tried to get her neediest students into the summer-school program. Cindy, Stefanie, and Manette needed the extra instruction desperately, she felt, and should unquestionably repeat first grade. Curtis, Trevor, Tasha, and Melissa also needed summer school, Donna thought, and should be held back if they made no progress in July and August.

Decisions about summer school were supposed to be based on three factors: a student's standardized test scores (or, in the case of first-graders, ECLAS scores), overall academic performance, and attendance. Tasha, Cindy, and Stefanie could qualify for summer school based on their shoddy attendance alone, Donna realized with some relief. It was comforting to think they would have one more shot—five weeks with another, possibly more skillful teacher.

But a week after Donna had sent her list of summer-school candidates to Brenda Robertson, a school secretary called the classroom and asked for Cindy, Trevor, and Tasha to report downstairs. They had returned to class with taped envelopes, which Robertson had instructed them to give their mothers. Curious, Donna opened Cindy's letter and saw that it was recommending her for summer school. She was amazed—why hadn't she been informed of the decision, or better yet, been in on it? Why was it the administration's decision to make unilaterally, anyway, given how much better Donna knew these children and their abilities?

Above all, Donna wondered, why were the four other students whom she thought sorely in need of summer school being overlooked?

The school, in fact, was being allowed only one class of first-graders that summer: Despite the perceived push to end social promotion across the system, many at the Board of Ed still believed that holding back students in the earliest grades was too stigmatizing, and that summer school for such young children was a poor use of money. On paper, the board endorsed other services for the smallest struggling students, which were indeed preferable to grade retention: Tutoring, which some of Donna's students did get during Success for All and P.S. 92's after-school program, was the board's top recommendation. Small class size was another, but as Donna's experience made clear, it could not guarantee a novice teacher's success with her neediest students. Good, frequent counseling might help, too, but clearly that was hard to come by at schools like P.S. 92, where so many children were competing for the services of so few social workers and guidance counselors.

In Donna's mind, it wasn't nearly as traumatic to repeat a grade at age seven as at eleven, twelve, or thirteen. But when she questioned the decision to promote Curtis, Stefanie, and Manette to second grade with no summer school, the response was dismissive. Donna wondered how Stefanie's and Manette's second-grade teachers would take it when they arrived in September unable to string letters into the simplest words or recite the days of the week. It just wasn't right.

And yet her own promotion to the second year of teaching was just as automatic. In mid-June she received her year-end evaluation, a single piece of paper titled "Annual Professional Performance Review and Report on Probationary Service of Pedagogical Employee." Rahmaan and Robertson had summed up her performance with a single letter: S, for satisfactory. There was room on the page for comments, but they had not written any. Donna wanted more feedback, though after her various tangles with administrators that year, she was beginning to see the benefits of being left alone.

.   .   .

As the days grew longer and went faster, Donna's mind was on measuring her students' progress since September. One rainy Friday, the students of Room 218 wrote their last essays for the hallway bulletin board, summing up what they had learned in first grade. To Donna they sounded like poetry, tumbling and breathless and exuberant.

"I learned about reading books and ABCs and writing," Monique, the Haitian girl who'd arrived in January, wrote, "being smart and sitting right and I learned the rules and we learned how to count by 2s and we will walk, not run, and to do homework." She had written the essay just like she talked, blurting things out in no particular order but with great enthusiasm. The girl was a chatterbox, and all of Donna's attempts to quiet her down had failed. Still, Donna loved her ebullience. Like Stefanie's, it would carry her far.

Shakeela wrote: "I learned not to call out, and I learned to raise my hand, and I learned about good manners, and I learned about reading, and I learned about writing, and I learned how to sing, and I learned how to write neatly." Unlike Monique, Shakeela had also learned a thing or two about punctuation, Donna noted, as she hung their essays side by side after dismissal that afternoon. In the middle of the bulletin board, Donna had stapled a postcard of a lurid sunset.

Jamilla, who had decided she wanted to be a reporter, wrote: "In first grade I learned how to go to school and do my work and do the 5 W's, who, what, where, why, when. I love my Ms. Moffett I learn to be good and nice. I love to write."

"I learned to write about clouds," Briella had written, clearly referring to the storybooks that had come courtesy of Nina Wasserman. Donna felt a shiver of victory as she read the girl's essay, thinking back on her clash with Marie Buchanan over reading materials. "Ms. Moffett is fun. I learned to be student of the month. You are fun 1–218, I love you."

Even Melissa's sentences were upbeat, with no hint of the gloom and inertia that had so often swallowed her enthusiasm. "I learned how to read books," she wrote. "I learned how to do math and I learned how to do my homework. I learned to dance. I love my class 1–218."

Nicole had written an ode to Donna. "I learned to have a beautiful teacher and I learned to read and write, and write a love letter to my teacher, and math and I learned to follow the rules, and art. And, I learned . . ." She had stopped to think or dream and run out of time.

The essays spoke volumes about how much they had grown in first grade. Jamilla, who had arrived in Room 218 so moody and bored by schoolwork, had become so excited about writing that she talked about it as a career, carried a notebook in her pocket, and begged to go to the writing center—albeit to copy lines from her favorite books. Briella, whose writing had been almost illegible in September, was now much more careful and neat. Nicole, who could not spell anything without help last fall, was writing full sentences almost perfectly.

As a whole, the students' summaries of what they learned from Donna—"being smart and sitting right" and "I learn to be good and nice" and "I learned to read and write" and "I learned how to sing"—were the best she could have asked for. They reflected her most heartfelt goals, and helped her believe that she had not been such an awful teacher, after all. Briella's final sentence—"You are fun 1–218, I love you"—was the sugar on top.

But looking at the official list of what every first-grader should be able to do by June, Donna could not feel nearly as satisfied. The list, written by New York City education officials and based on the state's curriculum standards, was four pages long, in tiny print. The school had sent it home with every student in September to spell out exactly what was expected of students, partly so parents could not complain if their child was held back at year's end.

Donna could check off quite a few reading and writing standards that several students had made great progress on, and that some had mastered. Nicole now chose to go to the story corner during learning center time, pulling a few books off the shelves and sounding out the words with the awkward grace of a new reader. Jamilla was reading and writing beautifully. Even Curtis was able to recognize and sound out many more letters than in September, though he still could not read.

Yet for every triumph, there was a nagging failure. By the end of first grade, all Donna's students were supposed to "read a range of materials, including poems, picture books, letters and simple informational books," according to the list. They should be able to "recognize by sight at least 150 words they see often when reading," "add to a rapidly growing vocabulary," and "choose four or more books to read every day alone or with help."

But Cindy and Manette could not read or write a single word on the Early Childhood Literacy Assessment System, prompting Donna to write on their score sheets: "Needs basic skills and remediation urgently!"

Stefanie recognized only five of the forty-two words on ECLAS, up from one (*up*) in November. For another part of the assessment, which asked her to write about a story Donna had read aloud, Stefanie copied sentences off a Success for All poster on a nearby wall: "Help and encourage others to practice active listening. Everyone participates. Explain your ideas and tell why."

Later that day, she had complained bitterly of hunger, reminding Donna that her own limitations were not the only reason behind Stefanie's academic troubles. "I need some food *now*," she said, begging for a snack.

Certainly Stefanie's extenuating circumstances—her perpetual hunger and stomachaches, her frequent absences, her volatile home life, and her mother's struggle with English—factored heavily into her lack of progress in first grade. But had Donna's inexperience played as much, if not more, of a role? If she had been better at executing lessons, staying on schedule, and addressing each child's weaknesses, Stefanie might have had more of a fighting chance. If she had pestered Stefanie's mom, who had skipped both parent-teacher conferences, Donna might have at least convinced her to send Stefanie to school more often.

In math, Donna's students should have learned to "count forward and backward by ones and twos up to 100," "show an understanding of fractions," "identify three-dimensional shapes," and "create and solve word problems." And that was just the beginning.

Even now, Donna was galloping through math lessons, trying to cover as many first-grade standards as possible. An exercise in which the kids cut out cylinders, cubes, prisms, and spheres went all right—until they had to write descriptions of each shape. The more advanced students, like Manuel and Angelique, did fine, but Nicole left hers blank and Briella missed the point completely. "Cube is my favorite," she wrote. "Cylinder I love them, them is fun."

Donna had to wonder: Why did first-graders need to know what prisms and spheres were, anyway? It was over the top—an example of overreaching in the attempt to prove expectations were high for all students. In another example, a homework assignment that asked Donna's students to write their own word problems was so complicated that many left it blank. Some kids' parents tried to do it for them, but they did not understand the assignment themselves. This was not so much a failing of Donna's or P.S. 92's, but of the system for choosing a math program that required intensive training that it could not afford, or find enough time for, let alone experts to do the training, and of New York State for setting unrealistic goals. As usual in large, churning school systems, there were so many parties to blame and so many cushions for failure that no one had to accept responsibility.

The second weekend in June, Donna sat at her dining room table and planned one last festivity: an awards ceremony at which every student would be honored. Every last one of them had improved some aspect of his or herself during first grade, and Donna wanted to celebrate these victories. She pictured a pomp-and-circumstance atmosphere in Room 218, the children listening solemnly as she described their successes and beaming as they received their awards. She had bought certificates at a teacher supply store, bright pink with AWARD WINNER stamped boldly across them. On a whim, Donna had also bought twenty pairs of socks, frilly and colorful for the girls, sporty for the boys. Maybe for a while, they would think of her when they put them on. Every day now, she was telling them how much she loved them and how they were the best first-grade class ever.

"For the rest of my life, I will never forget any of you," she said one afternoon as they all fanned themselves in the humid terrarium of a classroom. She was certain she never would.

Now and then she also found herself reminding them not to forget *her*.

"I hope you'll come say hello to me when you're in second grade," she had said a few times. "I hope that some of you will become my special helpers when I have a new class of first-graders who need smart older children to look up to."

She held the awards ceremony on June 21, after the kids had finished their morning writing assignment (*L.O.: We will write about summer*). There were only four school days left. Like so many of Donna's other expectations that year, her dream of a dignified ceremony did not come to fruition. The students were scooting around the room in their seats, giggling and saying, "I'm thirsty!" Maybe they thought it was party time—or, more likely, they sensed the finality of what was about to take place, and it made them fidget.

When Donna finally got them quiet, she took out the pink certificates and bag of socks and took a seat by the window.

"I think that I can clearly say that you all worked very, very hard this year in first grade," she said, trying to look into all twenty pairs of eyes. She summoned Cindy first, and the girl shuffled over with the dazed, slightly sheepish look she had worn all year.

"You, my dear, deserve to be commended because you stopped crying every day and you stopped having temper tantrums and you stopped ripping the posters off the walls." Cindy, always eager for new possessions, tried to grab her award packet. But Donna caught her hand and pumped it, making Cindy grin and show the gap where her missing front teeth had been.

Manette came next. "I want to commend you, Manette, for learning to write letters and make words and always trying very hard," Donna said, shaking Manette's hand and giving her a packet. She commended Mariah for getting 100 on every spelling test; Shane for doing his homework far more often now than at the beginning of the year; Shakeela for being the best reader; Curtis, who had never stopped drawing sharks and monsters, for being the best artist.

When it was Nicole's turn, Donna reached for a shopping bag that she had hidden under her desk. Nicole's eyes widened as she realized that whatever was inside was for her, and she smiled as the others looked on enviously.

"If we had to pick a top student who has had excellent behavior all year long and done excellent work, who was never once late, never once sent to time out, it would be Nicole Peat." She dipped a hand into the shopping bag and pulled out a small denim jacket decorated with suns, stars, and crescent moons. "Ooooh," the students said as Donna placed the jacket around Nicole's shoulders.

Stefanie was the last to be called. "Stefanie is being rewarded because she stopped screaming and hitting and learned how to use self-control and because she tries so hard," Donna announced. The girl jumped into Donna's lap, placed an arm around her neck, and grinned at her class, her chipmunk cheeks puffing out. Since she seemed to be settling in, Donna asked if she felt like making a speech.

Gone were the days when Stefanie would have responded by screaming or grabbing Donna's chalk. She thought for a moment, a finger on her lips, then said something that pointed up both Donna's successes and her failures.

"I love my class," the girl said. "And I want to learn how to read and write."

.   .   .

Donna wanted to believe that even a decade of teaching experience would not have helped her much with Stefanie or Manette, but it was blasphemy to think that way. Just a few weeks earlier, in late May, Congress had passed President Bush's No Child Left Behind law, which would present failing schools nationwide with the kind of sanctions that New York City already imposed. The law would require all public schools to test students annually starting in third grade, as New York already did. Those whose test scores remained low would supposedly face closure—as P.S. 92 already had—and their students would theoretically get the choice of transferring to a better school. Blaming the failures of children like Stefanie on poverty or their parents was becoming verboten in America. They were nobody's fault but the public schools'—a position that sounded appealingly tough in political sound bites, but felt maddeningly empty now that Donna was no longer judging the school system from the outside.

Bush was also requiring poor urban schools, which got a lot of federal money, to use "scientifically proven" methods of teaching reading. And while the administration was careful not to tout any particular programs, Success for All was a clear favorite. Donna had grown accustomed to the syncopated rhythms of Success for All, yet she still hated the lockstep approach and stopwatch mentality. In the second week of June, she mischievously asked her class their opinion of Success for All, and the responses had been almost uniformly negative. Shakeela said, "It's boring," and quiet Mariah said she disliked Success for All because "I don't get to stay with Ms. Moffett." Even Tasha, who usually disdained academic discussions, offered an astute observation: "I don't like reading the same books over and over."

Maybe when a teacher was brand new in the classroom, with no tools for teaching reading, such a mechanized approach was the safest bet. Donna had to concede that possibility now that she saw how complicated learning to read was for children who had not been read to at home, or even spoken to in proper English. She also saw now that consistency was important for young children, especially those who had little or none at home, and that the routines of Success for All provided it. But she also hoped—no, fiercely believed—that such regimentation could be softened to good effect. Children had to be allowed to laugh now and then throughout the day, to be surprised, to wiggle around and use their imaginations.

And shouldn't teachers be allowed to follow their instincts now and then instead of a script? So many times, Nina Wasserman had told Donna that the best teachers in a school like P.S. 92 were the ones who could blend their own personality and ideas with the rigid curriculum in a way that enhanced rather than flouted it. With a few more years of finding her way, Donna hoped she could master that difficult art—if, in fact, she could stick it out at P.S. 92 that long.

Though the Teaching Fellows program required Donna to stay at P.S. 92 for two years, Nina was already urging her to move to a higher-performing school after getting her master's degree. Nina thought she'd be happier in a school where risk-taking and individuality were embraced, and that was small enough for the principal to work closely with the teachers. She thought Donna would fit in much better at a more progressive school—one that took a more relaxed approach to teaching reading because it did not have to fixate on preparing students for standardized tests.

But the teaching fellows were not meant to work in such schools—Donna couldn't get that out of her head. The point of the program was to make sure *every* child in New York City got a sound education, and though she was not as bullish about the prospect as she had been nine months earlier, Donna still wanted, needed to be part of the movement. Nina was probably right—she *would* be happier, day to day, in a school that was not so "hooked on phonics." But at this point, Donna flatly rejected the idea of abandoning P.S. 92 despite its rigidity and the limitations it entailed. She wanted to see Nicole, Stefanie, and the others graduate from fifth grade—to follow their progress from year to year and support them as they moved through elementary school. Working elsewhere might be more comfortable, but comfort had not been her goal when she applied to the program, she stubbornly reminded herself. She would not abandon the cause.

.   .   .

For now, though, the twenty students that Donna had nurtured through this year were the only ones who were real to her—the only ones who mattered. As the year wound down, she began looking for ways to keep looking out for them after they left Room 218. After school on June 19, as a miniature fan she'd bought at a ninety-nine-cent store ruffled her hair, Donna sat at one of the little tables, studying a computer printout of her class roster. After having so little control over so many decisions affecting her students, she had been surprised to learn that she'd get to recommend which teachers they would have for second grade.

She studied the list like a puzzle, tapping her pencil on one name, then another. Though most of the second-grade teachers worked just down the hall, she had not found the time to get to know them or their strengths well. So instead of mulling which teacher would be best for each child, she thought about which kids should stay together next year and which should not.

Off the bat, Donna put Shane and Patrick in separate classes.

They talked and fooled around too much, and Shane seemed a bad influence on Patrick. She assigned Patrick to Room 204, Ms. Martinez, and Shane to Room 205, Ms. Talbot. Nicole's was the next name she focused on. Who would look out for sad, stick-figured Nicole when she was no longer under Donna's protective eye? Scanning the list, she decided that Shakeela, absent-minded but fundamentally sweet, had motherly instincts and would provide comfort to Nicole in September. She put the two of them with Shane, and added chatty Monique, whom she wanted to separate from the equally talkative Manette and Briella. In all, Donna assigned four children to Ms. Talbot, five to Ms. Greco, and six to Ms. Martinez, making sure each teacher got at least one of her strongest students and one of her weakest.

Two of the boys, including Manuel, who was moving back to the Bronx, were switching schools in the fall. As for the remaining three—Curtis, Stefanie, and Melissa—Robertson had taken it on herself to choose their new teachers, since they'd been some of Donna's most perplexing students. All three would be going to classrooms where none of their Room 218 classmates had been assigned.

Eenie, meenie, minie, mo. This divvying up felt too casual, too random—just as the parents should have felt entrusting their children to Donna that first day of school. Would other teachers treat Nicole as tenderly? Would they look past Stefanie's wild bids for attention and appreciate her vivacity and humor? Would they be more patient with Melissa's moods, less tolerant of Curtis's weird outbursts?

It was a crapshoot—though less of one than her students had been subjected to this year. Donna was still an unknown when they were being assigned to first-grade classrooms the previous

June. None of their kindergarten teachers or parents had any idea of her strengths and weaknesses, or how well her personality would mesh with those of her students. Donna had not even heard of the Teaching Fellows program at that point—she was planning Gerry's trip to London, making sure his days went smoothly. Now she was trying to make sure that twenty lives got off to a good, fair start, and hoping that she had not messed up too badly.

.   .   .

There was, by the fourth week of June, a heady sense of finality and imminent, enormous change. Though Donna had not lived by the public school calendar in almost thirty years, the feelings and rituals associated with the last weeks of class were forever imprinted in her brain—just as they are for most of us. There was the packing up of books, the dismantling of wall decorations, the cleaning out of grimy desks—knowing all would be unpacked, re-hung, reoccupied in two short months. It was a lovely contrast: The comforting certainty everything would begin again in September, mixed with the sense of possibility that only summer evokes. Donna had missed these feelings as an adult, and reliving them felt gorgeously dreamlike, joyful, and melancholy, never quite real.

One afternoon, Donna found a computer printout in her mailbox with twenty mysterious names: Esmerelda, Luvelle, Samsara, Chrismye. These would be her students in September—her second first-grade class. For now, she had no photographs to study, no faces to memorize or habits to mull. There were only the names, followed a few days later by the "cumes," or files that accompanied each child from grade to grade.

The art teacher, Lisa Fischer, visited Room 218 during the last week of school to leaf through the cumes with Donna. Fischer, a wisecracking young woman who had been at P.S. 92 for a few years, went down the list of students and offered a thumbnail sketch of each. "She's real sweet," she said, "but he's got nothing upstairs." Another was "a hellion," in Fischer's estimation, while yet another was a combination of Cindy and Manette.

A few other teachers had warned Donna that she was getting some major behavior problems next year, and she worried that she was being dumped on. It was indeed a nasty trick that some teachers and principals used on colleagues they did not like. But in this case, as Donna would learn with pride in the fall, she had gained a reputation of working well with disruptive students.

"I feel like I am beaten down and I have to keep getting up over and over and over again," she complained to Paul Herbold, the computer teacher, the morning after Fischer's visit. She wanted to ask Rahmaan about her new class, but Herbold wisely counseled her not to judge the new students until she could see them in action.

"Wait till September," he said. Only then would Donna learn that in fact, several of the students described as horrors would thrive in Room 218, and that, though she hadn't believed it possible, another class could be as compelling as the one that had confounded and charmed her that first year.

.   .   .

On June 27, the last day of school, Donna was already sweating as she marched seventeen of her students—Stefanie, Tasha, and Cindy were no-shows, predictably—upstairs for the last time. By this point the weather was wiltingly hot, and almost everyone had abandoned their uniforms for shorts and tank tops or thin dresses. They had all grown an inch or two since September, Donna noticed, and a few, like Briella and Melissa, had lost some of the baby fat they came in with.

Donna's students could tell that their teacher wanted everything to go perfectly on this bright, steamy morning. This made some, like Trevor, antsy, and others, like Briella and Melissa, a little shy. She had been saying goodbye to them for weeks, in all kinds of ways. So today, for the real goodbye, they were not sure what to expect. The walls of Room 218 were half bare, and it no longer felt like the warm, safe place they had inhabited for nine months.

Manuel's mother came for him early—she had sent him to school just to fetch his report card, which had all Es, for excellent. They were leaving the women's shelter and going home to the Bronx. Donna wondered if she would ever again see Manuel, one of her favorite, smartest students.

She had thought up her own literacy lesson, even though school ended at noon that day. *L.O.: Students will discuss how to stay safe this summer.*

"Boys and girls, don't make me angry," Donna warned as she wrote summer safety rules on the board.

1. Always cross only *at the corner*.
2. Never cross in the middle of the block.
3. Wait for the WALK sign.
4. Look both ways!

Donna had gotten carried away, preparing this lesson. "Never eat or drink any cleaning products!" she wrote as the children copied obediently. "Never touch animals you do not know! Tell an adult right away if you get scratched or bitten!" As always, what she wanted most was to protect them. And more than ever, now that they were leaving Room 218 for good, she could do it only in a surface-skimming way.

She had stuffed their report cards with compliments and advice for this third, final marking period, even though the higher-ups had urged her to "keep it brief," just as they had on Donna's evaluation form. The more Donna gushed about a student, they had said, the more his or her parents could complain if a future teacher was more critical.

She took the students to the story corner as the end came near. But as they started to talk casually about their summer plans, she felt a rush of despair. Soon they would be gone. A few tears leaked from her eyes, and though she quickly brushed them away, some students spotted them.

"She faking?" Trevor asked dubiously.

"No, she really crying!" Briella marveled.

Nicole, who had been even quieter than usual that morning, brought Donna a tissue, just as Donna had so often done for her. "I don't want a different teacher," she whispered, shifting from foot to foot. "I want Ms. Moffett forever."

Melissa's mom was the next to arrive, and Melissa, for one, looked happier than usual. While Donna went over her report card with Rose, Melissa circled the room, shaking hands with her classmates as Donna had taught her. "I love my class, 1–218," she had written for the bulletin board, and she did seem genuinely fond of each boy and girl as she pumped their hands. One last hug for Donna, who'd had such a hard time understanding Melissa for most of the year, and the girl was gone.

Donna would probably never know what long-term effect, if any, she would have on Melissa and the other students. One or two might keep in touch with her over the years, if she was lucky. But most would be lost to her forever after they or she left P.S. 92. Even next year, when they were just down the hall or upstairs, there was no guarantee that she would see them.

Her colleague Deborah Ben-Ari had said, "Being a teacher is like giving birth to twenty children every single year." But while your "family" doubled every year, the first set of kids left you after nine months, never to be in your care again. How irrevocable each class of students was. What a strange, searing loss to endure.

Then it was noon, time for the students to take the contents of their desks and go. Monique let out a cheer. Trevor announced he did not want to part with shy, pretty Mariah. "I want to go home with her and live with her," he said, as Mariah looked mortified. Briella, who had been crying because Melissa forgot to shake hands with her, wrote a farewell message on the blackboard: "I will mis Ms. Moffett."

Donna brightened briefly as parent after parent—eleven in all—came to fetch their children and tell her goodbye. Some, including Curtis and his mother Liana, disappeared while Donna was talking to others. Jamilla's mom hugged Donna tightly, and Angelique's gave her a kiss. By now, she was buzzing with nervous energy and emotion that she should, but could not, contain. Her gestures—bending her knees to look each student in the eye, clutching her hands to her chest—were dramatic, and the students were wary. Especially Nicole.

Donna, too, was nervous about saying goodbye to Nicole. When Mr. Peat arrived shortly after noon, she distracted herself by reading him the girl's report card. Donna had given Nicole Es in every subject, when last marking period she had gotten only Gs in math, science, and reading.

"Consistently throughout the year, Nicole's behavior and academic work have been outstanding," she read, as Nicole looked more uncomfortable by the second. "She is reading and writing beautifully and has strong math skills. Nicole has tremendous promise and is sure to succeed in all she tackles. Her character is truly an inspiration, and she deserves the best in life!"

At the end was an olive branch to Nicole's aunt Anna, who Donna knew worked at Kings County Hospital. "If Nicole does follow in auntie's footsteps to become a great doctor or nurse, her patients will be very fortunate," Donna had written.

As she read her own comments aloud, Donna's voice cracked and she started to cry once again. Only a few students were left in the classroom, and most looked incredulous. Jamilla clicked her tongue like an embarrassed teenager. Nicole stared at her teacher for a few seconds, frozen, then began crying herself. It was her father's leg that she buried her head in, not Donna's, as she tried to muffle her sobs. She was still crying softly as her father led her out a minute later, unable to say goodbye.

Donna knew that crying was unprofessional, and felt terrible. But Nicole had been like a daughter to her that year. Had she done more for Donna than Donna had for Nicole? Nicole loved her intensely and unconditionally, as almost no one else had ever done. Donna had taken exquisite pleasure in Nicole's model behavior and academic progress, when so many of her classmates had consistently crushed Donna's high expectations and made her feel like a failure. Even Nicole's neediness that year, while a constant source of worry, made Donna feel important and beloved when so much else about teaching had made her feel worthless.

But now, the daily affection that Donna had showered on Nicole would disappear from the girl's life. She had rattled

Nicole by crying, confirming her fear that something precious was about to be lost. As children shouted and boom boxes blared and an ice cream truck played its jangly tune outside her windows, Donna added "keep composure on last day of school" to the long mental list of goals for her second year.

·   ·   ·

She had so much to do in her classroom—or rather, to undo—that she missed P.S. 92's last-day luncheon for teachers. For once, there was no Brooklyn College class to get to, no SFA lesson to practice, nothing imminent to worry about as she fussed over Room 218, the activity that had so often calmed her that year. At the law firm, Donna had been an empty-inbox person who kept her surroundings free of color or clues about herself. Here, she was a packrat whose personality was practically spray-painted around her room. Hard to believe that eleven months earlier, she had packed her possessions at Flemming, Zulack into a single box.

Her desk alone was a crowded petri dish, growing all kinds of interesting things: her lesson book, worn now, and a stubby piece of pink chalk. A paperweight, two empty milk cartons, and a broken pencil, probably Trevor's. A coffee cup with the inscription, "Behind every boss is a great secretary." The squirrel music box that Julian had given her, which would not play its warped "Für Elise" again until fall. Piles of children's books, a ruler, and some glittery stickers. A box of colored paper clips, a tiny clock, and a Styrofoam cup of cold coffee. A bottle of hand disinfectant, and a photo of Melissa and Shakeela with their arms around each other. A love letter from Manuel, with a picture he'd drawn of Donna. He had colored her skin a creamy brown, the same shade as his.

Now she had to stow it all away, and it felt odd—like stowing away her identity for the summer. Who would Donna Moffett be from June 28 through August 27—just another New Yorker enduring summer in the city, with no one but herself to worry about? It was impossible to imagine how she'd feel or what she'd do when she woke up the next morning. One thing was certain, though: She'd return to P.S. 92 for a few more hours, to pack up a few last things.

She did not feel the need to finish today.

EPILOGUE

Since July 2001, when I wrote my last article about Donna Moffett for the *New York Times*, public schools in New York City and nationwide have experienced some of the most rapid, dramatic changes in their history.

President Bush has pushed ahead with his No Child Left Behind law, which has rightly won praise for drawing attention to the glaring achievement gap between white and minority students, middle-class and poor. For the first time, all schools have to break down testing data so the performance of special-education students, those who can't speak English well, those living in poverty, and other historically troubled groups is spotlighted. This is an important, necessary change.

Yet the law has also generated protest that grows louder and spreads farther by the month. Schools, teachers' unions, and even governors complain that No Child Left Behind is too relentlessly focused on raising test scores, setting goals that are impossible to meet and of questionable worth. Almost a third of American public schools have been labeled "in need of improvement" for not meeting yearly achievement targets, including many whose reputations are good. In many cases, schools just barely miss their targets because a handful of students were absent on testing days, or scored a few points too low. Too often, such mundane technicalities give the law a bad rap, providing fodder for complainers who would rather see it fail than have it reflect badly on them and their schools.

Another widespread complaint is that schools are not getting the money they need to comply with the law; indeed, the Bush administration allotted $6 billion less than the $18 billion Congress authorized in federal antipoverty funds for poor schools in 2003–04. As usual, many pundits are saying those schools don't need more money, pointing to examples like the District of Columbia, which spends well over $10,000 per student yet still disappoints.

Most schools *do* need more money than they're getting to meet the goals of No Child Left Behind, but they also need to be extraordinarily thoughtful and creative in planning how to spend it. This remains a huge challenge in urban schools, which have too few smart, enterprising administrators making decisions, and too few savvy, dedicated teachers to execute sound instructional changes. Because schools have to invest so much time and money in math and reading, other subjects are languishing, especially in schools that are not artful or agressive enough to raise outside funds or win grants. Art, music, home economics, and foreign languages are among the classes getting squeezed, too often losing their time and budget slots to test preparation. This is shameful, though a return to the old days, when standardized tests were easier and schools faced no real sanctions for poor performance, would be, too. The challenge, more pressing than ever, is to ensure all children learn the fundamentals while still cultivating their creativity and curiosity.

High-poverty schools in particular have not yet found a happy medium, and the need is dire.

In response to swelling objections—including those from over a dozen states that were threatening to flout the law—the Bush administration began loosening some regulations in 2003–04. Test scores of recent immigrants who do not speak English, for example, no longer factor into whether a school is meeting annual targets for academic progress. More significant, and more troubling for some needy schools, is a loosening of the rule requiring a "highly qualified teacher" in every classroom by June 2006. The change gives small, rural districts more leeway.

In truth, many educators already considered the teacher rule something of a joke, since it counted teachers like Donna Moffett, who came in through alternative training programs like the Teaching Fellows, as "highly qualified" from the get-go. But like New York State, which in 2000 accepted Harold Levy's argument that career-changers who won acceptance to competitive programs like the Teaching Fellows could handle their own classrooms off the bat, the Bush administration has put great stock in alternate-route teachers. And so their ranks have grown rapidly: Florida alone, with a booming school-age population and only about six thousand new education-school graduates a year, is hiring thousands of teachers like Donna to help fill up to twenty thousand annual vacancies.

The Bush administration and others point to the Teaching Fellows program as an enviable model, and some of the nation's most troubled school districts, like Los Angeles, Washington, D.C., and New Orleans, have adopted it. But while that program has improved with time, other alternate-route programs springing up are of dubious quality. Too often, the professors are weak, promised mentors never materialize, and career-changers are dispatched to schools that resent their presence and riddle them with petty hostilities. At the same time, too many career-changers prove fickle, quitting after their first few run-ins with administrators, parents, or students. The problem was especially acute during the recession that followed the 2001 terrorist attacks, when teaching became a last resort for thousands of people who could not find other work.

Though the recession effectively ended the teacher shortage that had New York and other urban school systems so panicked in 2000, I suspect it brought many people into teaching who weren't truly committed to the cause. It remains to be seen how many will stay and excel.

.   .   .

In New York, the changes spurred by No Child Left Behind have almost been eclipsed by a more radical development: the state legislature's decision in 2002 to abolish the Board of Education and give the new mayor, Michael Bloomberg, direct control over the city school system. Bloomberg had campaigned on the promise that if he won control, the system would be freed from the political infighting that so often thwarted change. Only Bloomberg, and a chancellor whom he alone picked, could be blamed for its failures.

Bloomberg replaced Harold Levy with Joel Klein, a plainspoken lawyer who headed the antitrust division of the Justice Department under Bill Clinton. Another chancellor out, another in—but this time, the mayor and chancellor would act as one instead of fighting over differences of opinion and style. Principals and teachers were hopeful, if nervous. Mayoral control of the

schools had always seemed a pipe dream, yet here it was, and the
nation was watching in fascination. Could the dream of making
New York schools enviable become reality, too?

Bloomberg warned that improvements would come slowly
and with great tumult. Sure enough, the 2002–03 and 2003–04
school years were awash in chaos, anger, and confusion. The
teachers finally got their raises in June 2002—starting salaries
increased to $39,000 from $31,900—which went a long way toward helping Klein find eight thousand new teachers that fall.
Remarkably, 85 percent of the new hires in 2002–03 were certified, the highest rate in decades. Many of those counting as certified, though—about 1,800—were teaching fellows, basically
coming in cold.

Like President Bush, Bloomberg and Klein came up with an
unimpeachable name for the reform plan they quickly designed:
Children First. Neither man had a whit of education experience,
but like Harold Levy before them, they touted their success in
the corporate and legal worlds (Bloomberg's media company
had made him a billionaire, and Klein had gone from the Justice
Department to Bertelsmann, Inc., an arm of the German media
conglomerate) as an advantage. They thought Board of Ed
holdovers would not necessarily share their fervor for change,
and hired a whole new team—mostly from the business world—
to help carry out their revolution. One by one, career educrats
who had worked for three, four, even seven chancellors, cleaned
out their desks. Some took with them an acceptance of the status quo that would not be missed. But collectively, they also took
the kind of deep institutional knowledge that takes decades to
build in a system so large and complex.

Out, too, went dozens of instructional programs, some of
which had unquestionably been helping troubled schools im-

prove. In their place, Bloomberg and Klein imposed uniform reading and math curriculums that all but the top-performing schools had to use—an enormous change, and daunting to execute in nearly one thousand schools at once. It would be the first time in decades that the vast majority of city schools would have the same textbooks, lesson plans, and schedules, and that all eighty thousand teachers would be trained in a single approach. The idea was worthy: In particular, it was meant to address the huge problem of students and teachers moving often from school to school, and having to start over with a whole new curriculum. But in the short term, at least, the new programs have broken any instructional consistency that existed—the best example being in the Chancellor's District, with Success for All and Math Trailblazers.

Despite the fact that many schools using Success for All—including P.S. 92—had seen their test scores rise, the system's new instructional leaders thought the program was not only too expensive, but too regimented and frustrating for teachers. Klein and Bloomberg also thought the Chancellor's District itself was too expensive to maintain, and disbanded it in 2003. Under the new curriculum, children at P.S. 92 and others formerly in the special district still get at least ninety minutes of reading and writing instruction a day, as do most students citywide. But the new programs are trickier for new teachers to get the hang of. Interestingly, they are also much more in the progressive-education mold than rigid programs like Success for All, emphasizing activities like "guided reading," in which a teacher works with one small group of readers while other small groups work independently.

Klein's chosen reading program put New York at the center of the national reading wars, which it had managed to avoid through several other chancellor's tenures. Traditionalist education pundits rained scorn on the decision to shun hard-core phonics programs like Success for All, and the Bush administration threatened to withhold No Child Left Behind funds from New York if it did not go with a program scientifically proven to help impoverished, struggling students. Klein ultimately bowed to the pressure and substituted a more traditionalist phonics program in the lowest-performing schools, though he kept the larger "balanced literacy" (read: progressive) component.

I felt a mix of emotions as these changes emerged, at a time when I was leaving the education beat, and New York, for a new assignment as a national reporter in Miami. As much as I disliked the monotony of Success for All, with its uninspired, staccato-beat stories and tension-inducing teacher script, I had begun to believe in its approach—at least for the most inexperienced teachers and most academically fragile students. A strict phonics program should unequivocally be paired with more creative lessons using children's literature, just as P.S. 92 and other Chancellor's District schools tried to do with their afternoon reading period. That's essential, it seems, in keeping teachers fulfilled and students curious. And I'd like to think that once children learn to read well, they can leave hard-core phonics programs in the dust.

My feelings about the dissolution of the Chancellor's District were more straightforward: I considered it a major loss. As maddening as the intense bureaucratic supervision could be, and the superficial rules and routines meant to lend the appearance of constant progress, the infusion of extra money into Chancellor's District schools guaranteed smaller classes, a longer school day, intensive whole-school reform programs, and other perks that were unquestionably helping students. Without their special district, P.S. 92 and other schools like it risk getting lost in the crowd once more.

·   ·   ·

One program that has survived the Bloomberg-Klein revolution, at least so far, is New York City Teaching Fellows. Klein—like Levy, an altruistic career-changer himself—not only embraced the program but increased its ranks, bringing in a record 2,400 new fellows in September 2003. More than nineteen thousand people applied that year, and in New York, where the program's ad campaign has expanded to the subway cars in which millions of people ride each day, it has become something of a household name. It is not an exaggeration to say that almost everyone I know in the city and its suburbs knows someone who has applied to or joined the Teaching Fellows program. While this is partly a function of the recession, it is also a testament to the program's pull on New Yorkers who want to change their life's course, and to the almost mystical pull of teaching as a potentially enriching, rewarding career.

The program has changed, though, in that it no longer sends most recruits to the worst schools. The first group's experiences were so traumatic, in general—and they had such a hard time succeeding in the crisis environment of Chancellor's District and other failing schools—that Harold Levy and Vicki Bernstein decided to assign most to more stable, though generally still troubled, schools in the years since. They could do so because the first class of fellows had helped end the certification crisis in failing schools, at least for the time being.

Levy hoped that after a few years in higher-performing schools, many fellows, idealistic as they were, would voluntarily transfer into failing schools. Klein, too, told me he envisioned "swat teams" of second- or third-year fellows, led by a veteran teacher, going into failing schools with a game plan for how to make a difference there. It sounds good, but I worry that not enough fellows would actually make such a move, given the choice. I also doubt such a plan would go over well with administrators at failing schools.

Though the first year of the Teaching Fellows program was the bumpiest, it has continued to experience growing pains, and to hemorrhage recruits who lose faith in the school system or just aren't strong enough to persevere. Of about 6,400 fellows hired since 2000, about 1,400, or 22 percent, had left as of September 2003. Of the 323 fellows who started teaching in September 2000, a little more than half remain.

Still, more than five thousand fellows are teaching in New York schools as of this writing—one of every fifteen city teachers. Harold Levy's hope that the fellows would become a staple of the teaching force is, on paper anyway, becoming reality. But are they helping to change the culture of troubled schools? Is the system accepting only high-caliber applicants, or is the quality of new fellows declining as the program grows? As yet there is no research to help answer these questions, though anecdotally, many principals now seem pleased to have fellows in their schools. One change that they like is that incoming fellows now get seven weeks of training, including four weeks of observing and co-teaching in summer school classrooms.

The school system has also stopped putting most fellows in elementary school classrooms, and instead uses them to fill pressing vacancies in middle and high schools, and in bilingual and special-education programs. About four hundred fellows were hired as math teachers this year, after a specialized training program for people who didn't major in math but had experience in related fields like accounting. That is a triumph for the program, and for the schools.

In a less popular development, Joel Klein cut the program's budget last year so that fellows now pay for part of their master's degree program. They contribute about $4,000 over two years through payroll deductions, making the program a little less expensive for the school system. Levy feared the change would deter many people from applying, and indeed, the numbers are down this year: about sixteen thousand applied, or 20 percent less than in 2003. Vicki Bernstein, who still heads the program, thinks the drop is mostly a reflection of the improving economy. She also said that while many people now decide to apply for the program after hearing about it through word of mouth, a surprisingly large number of applicants over the last two years—20 percent—said their interest was piqued by the subway ads. I suspect that, like "Sad Girl," they appeal to people's vanity and get them dreaming about what mark they could make on the world. My favorite goes like this: "You remember the name of your first-grade teacher. Who will remember yours?"

.   .   .

Which brings us to Donna Moffett and her students. Donna is still teaching first grade in Room 218, a testament not only to her strength, but to her love for P.S. 92. In difficult times—and there have been many, despite the confidence and skill she has developed over four years of teaching—Donna thinks of the satisfaction she'll get from watching her first group of students graduate from fifth grade. Most of them will do so next June, departing for middle school and a whole new set of hurdles.

Donna earned her master's in teaching in May 2003, after three years of coursework that occasionally imparted sound wisdom but was often disappointingly dry or beside the point. She has occasionally yearned to try teaching another grade—second, maybe, or third—but her superiors at P.S. 92 urged her to stay put for a while. She got much better at teaching math and reading in her second year, and has been able to focus more thought and energy on science, social studies, and other subjects. Reading remains her favorite subject, though she has also cultivated a love of writing in her students, helping them create books and setting time aside for them to read their work to each other.

Public School 92 also steadily improved while it was in the Chancellor's District: 36.8 percent of its tested students met state standards in reading in 2002–03, up from 27.5 percent in Donna's first year on the job. In math, the progress has been even more striking: 37.1 percent of tested students met standards in 2002–03, up from 18.5 percent in 2000–01. The school had improved enough to leave the Chancellor's District even before the district was disbanded. This past year, though, as New York City schools abandoned their instructional programs and techniques for new ones the Klein team sanctioned, P.S. 92's fourth-grade reading scores plummeted for the first time in years. Only 25 percent of the school's fourth graders met reading standards in 2003–4, down from almost 44 percent the previous year. Middle School 2, just down the street and where many of Donna's first students will likely enroll as sixth-graders next fall, was also struggling: only 15.6 percent of its eight-graders met reading standards.

Though she couldn't imagine loving any group of students more than Curtis, Nicole, and the rest, the students in Donna's second class surprised her, proving themselves every bit as compelling. One morning early in her second year, a boy who had been assigned to another class noticed Donna playfully interacting with her students on the playground and was intrigued. "I want that teacher," he told his mother on the spot. The woman asked that her son be switched to Donna's classroom, and he turned out to be one of Room 218's brightest, most eager students that year.

Donna was assigned a different assistant principal in her second year, when Brenda Robertson went to work with the fourth-grade teachers, and to yet another in her third. Diana Rahmaan recently finished her fifth year as principal of P.S. 92—a remarkably long tenure for the leader of a beleaguered urban school. Jim Raffel, the other teaching fellow who started at P.S. 92 with Donna, transferred to a Manhattan high school after his first year to teach history, and loves it.

Nina Wasserman, Donna's Brooklyn College mentor and spiritual adviser, had a relapse of breast cancer in 2002 and died that December, leaving a great void in the lives of Donna and her many other protégés. Donna, who spoke at Nina's memorial service, misses her calm wisdom and nurturing, but perhaps in one way, Nina's absence has made Donna's path clearer. Nina felt strongly that Donna should move to another school with a more relaxed atmosphere and progressive approach. Donna could see her point and was sometimes tempted when Nina described the creative energy that defined schools like P.S. 321, a progressive bastion in affluent Park Slope, Brooklyn. But her stubborn dedication to P.S. 92 always bubbled up when she thought about leaving. "This is where I belong," she likes to say.

As for the students Donna taught that first year, many have made frequent visits to her classroom as they have grown older and taller, while others—including some she never would have expected to lose touch with—have drifted from her life. Curtis in particular has enjoyed coming back during his lunch hour or after school, helping Donna water her classroom plants and talking about what's going on in his life. She thinks he might be a scientist or botanist one day and feels confident about his future. Shakeela, Briella, and Angelique have also been regular visitors to Room 218, where Donna enlists their help passing out snacks or worksheets.

Surprisingly, Nicole Peat barely sought out Donna's company after first grade, perhaps because she knew the bond they had shared as student and teacher was irrevocable. She did, however, return to Room 218 for a Valentine's Day party in 2003, and sat at a now-too-small table with Shakeela, Briella, Angelique, Patrick, Shane, Trevor, and me. Shakeela split a ham-and-cheese sub from the bodega across the street into seven pieces, and they all talked cheerfully about missing Ms. Moffett, but liking third grade as much as first. Every one of them seemed to be growing into a kind, thoughtful, attentive, good-humored person. Every one seemed to exude qualities that Donna valued, and that she had tried so hard to instill in them that first year.

Stefanie and Manette continued to struggle academically, though one of their teachers told me in 2003 that Manette, in particular, was improving in reading. Stefanie was further behind, the teacher said, because of her still-frequent absences.

Manuel and Mariah left P.S. 92 after first grade; Manuel was returning home to the Bronx, and Mariah, like so many urban children, was continuing her nomadic journey through a series of schools, as her family moved once again. More recently, Cindy—who repeated first grade after all and did make progress learning to read the following year—left the school, as did Tasha. When Donna and I passed her in the hallway during one of my follow-up visits in 2002, she stared blankly when we greeted her.

I was visiting P.S. 92 one day in June 2002 when the school learned that a kindergartener had been murdered by his mother's boyfriend the previous night. According to the police, the man had drowned the boy in a bathtub after he spilled bubble bath on the floor, and then had strangled his mother, who was seven months pregnant. It turned out that the boy would have been in Donna's class the following year.

Was she just another anonymous New Yorker that summer, with a life as unknowable as anyone's who passes on the sidewalk in the city heat? That question was answered one day shortly after school ended, as Donna and her colleague Deborah Ben-Ari strolled on the Upper East Side of Manhattan after a shopping trip. A voice called her name as they passed an ice cream shop, and when she turned, confused, a man she did not recognize hurried out. "You were my daughter's teacher last year, Ms. Moffett," he said, offering her a free ice cream from the shop, where he worked. "She loved being in your class."

The whole city might have been blessing her, it felt so good.

ACKNOWLEDGMENTS

So many people contributed their time and wisdom to this book, but it was Donna Moffett, with all her candor, courage, and generosity of spirit, who made it possible. It was no small undertaking, for Donna—a private person unused to sharing her life with the world—was letting me watch as she took on an unthinkably difficult challenge. She gave me so much time and energy, even as she was drowning in endless new demands. She inspired me, frequently raised my spirits, and taught me so much about courage and conviction. I count her as a dear friend, and cannot adequately thank her for her participation.

Heartfelt thanks are also due to Diana Rahmaan, the principal of P.S. 92, who took a big chance in giving me regular access to her school, was always friendly and fair, and struck me as the model of grace under pressure. I deeply appreciate Brenda Robertson's tolerance and Marie Buchanan's openness while I wrote the newspaper series, and thank them and the other administrators and teachers at P.S. 92 for abiding my presence over time. Vera Pavone, with her keen historical perspective, was especially helpful, and Ruth Baptiste deserves singling out for her serenity and warmth.

Without Harold Levy, who trusted me and his vision for the Teaching Fellows program enough to sign off on my newspaper project, this book would never have taken shape. He was always generous with his time and insight, as were his colleagues Vicki Bernstein, Karla Oakley, Judith Rizzo, and Sandra Kase. Randi Weingarten, David Sherman, and Dick Riley at the United Federation of Teachers also lent their support and expertise, as did Jim Raffel, Frank Headley, Seth Teter, and many other teaching fellows I encountered over the years.

Donna's former bosses, Gerry Paul and Peter Flemming, provided me with valuable insight. I see now why they are so special to her.

At the *New York Times*, Joe Berger and Ethan Bronner, my talented editors on the education beat, made my articles about Donna Moffett sing and gave me the great blessing of time away from daily demands, so that I could visit P.S. 92 regularly. I am grateful for their endorsement of the book project, and for that of Bill Schmidt, Jennifer Preston, and others at the *Times*. Ozier Muhammad's striking photographs gave the newspaper series more of a soul. Many other colleagues provided advice and encouragement, especially Lawrence Downes, Jacques Steinberg, Dan Barry, Kate Zernike, and Andy Newman.

I feel lucky to have an agent, David McCormick, who saw the value of this project so early and kept rooting for it, with his dogged enthusiasm, even when the going got rough. Peter Osnos and Lisa Kaufman at PublicAffairs also believed in the book from start to finish, and Lisa's guidance and gentle, wise editing made it a lot better. And in the middle, Alice Truax saved the day with her talent and good humor, teaching me so much about book writing in one short, chaotic summer. Thanks, too, to John Firestone, for his top-notch advice.

Perhaps most steadying throughout this experience were a few loyal friends who gave much-needed moral support: Laura Pedrick, Dan Zegart, Nancy and Taylor Goodnough, Jon Romberg, Denise Rodgers, Kellianne Greenwood, Kate Phillips, and Sandi Haas, who also provided me with a lovely place to write. Kyle Haas, who witnessed the ups and downs of this project at closer range than anyone, has been unfailingly patient and encouraging. I love him for it.

Finally, Donna Moffett's students in her first year at P.S. 92, all twenty-six of them, made me experience a wider range of emotions than I thought possible, sometimes in a single day. They opened my mind and all my senses to the realities of being a child in a New York school, giving my beat a most human face and always teaching me something new. Like Donna, I'll always remember them all.

SELECTED BIBLIOGRAPHY

Archibold, Randal. "State Reports Disproportionate Number of Minority Pupils in Special Education," *New York Times*, February 3, 1999.

———. "Crew Outlines Plan To End Promotions For Failing Pupils," *New York Times*, June 10, 1999.

Berger, Joseph. "Albert Shanker, 68, Combative Leader Of Teachers, Dies," *New York Times*, February 23, 1997.

———. "The Odd Circle Of School Control; 'Power to the People' in 1960's Is Now Seen as 'Amateur Hour'," *New York Times*, June 16, 2002.

Celona, Larry and Ikimulisa Sockwell. "Bathtime Horror—Beau Kills Little Boy, Mom Over Spill: Cops," *New York Post*, June 26, 2002.

"Class Struggles: The UFT Story," *New York Teacher*, 1996.

Dillon, Sam. "Some School Districts Challenge Bush's Signature Education Law," *New York Times*, January 2, 2004.

———. "Bush Education Officials Find New Law a Tough Sell to States," *New York Times*, February 22, 2004.

———. "U.S. Set to Ease Some Provisions Of School Law," *New York Times*, March 14, 2004.

Freedman, Samuel G. *Small Victories: The Real World of a Teacher, Her Students, and Their High School* (New York: HarperPerennial, 1991).

Goodnough, Abby. "Wanted: Bored Professionals Who Have Teaching in Mind," *New York Times*, July 2, 2000.

———. "Education Chief Threatens Suit If Uncertified Teachers Remain," *New York Times*, July 18, 2000.

———. "Teacher Trainees Who Left Other Careers Speak of a Higher Calling," *New York Times*, August 1, 2000.

———. "Learning to Teach; A Novice's Hard Lesson: Bringing Order to a Class," *New York Times*, September 28, 2000.

———. "Fast-Track Certification Program For Teachers to Expand Tenfold," *New York Times*, October 14, 2000.

———. "Winnowing Process Begins for Novice Teachers," *New York Times*, November 22, 2000.

———. "Tears, Yes, but Triumphs, Too, for a Teacher," *New York Times*, December 11, 2000.

———. "The Ruling In The Schools: The Overview; State Judge Rules School Aid System Is Unfair To City," *New York Times*, January 11, 2001.

———. "20 Minds to Shape, 20 Mysteries to Plumb," *New York Times*, March 11, 2001.

———. "Teaching by the Book, No Asides Allowed," *New York Times*, May 23, 2001.

———. "'S' Is for Satisfactory, Not for Satisfied," *New York Times*, July 1, 2001.

———. "Interstate Competition for Teachers From Abroad," *New York Times*, July 18, 2001.

———. "Answering Call for Teachers, Some Find Only Frustration," *New York Times*, August 22, 2001.

———. "More Applicants Answer The Call For Teaching Jobs," *New York Times*, February 11, 2002.

———. "Views Differ About Aides In Classrooms," *New York Times*, May 19, 2003.

Greenhouse, Steven. "Tentative Pact for City Teachers Increases Pay, and Workweek," *New York Times*, June 11, 2002.

Hartocollis, Anemona. "Albany Tightens Standards For Teachers and Training," *New York Times*, September 18, 1999.

———. "The New, Flexible Math Meets Parental Rebellion," *New York Times*, April 27, 2000.

———. "Hiring of Teachers Is More Than a Matter of Decree," *New York Times*, September 2, 2000.

———. "As Social Status Sags, Teachers Call It a Career," *New York Times*, April 17, 2002.

Kozol, Jonathan. *Amazing Grace* (New York: Perennial, 1996).

———. *Ordinary Resurrections: Children in the Years of Hope* (New York: Perennial, 2001).

National Association of Colleges and Employers. "Fall 2000 Salary Survey."

National Commission on Excellence in Education. "A Nation At Risk," Washington, DC: U.S. Government Printing Office, April 1983.

Lehman, Nicholas. "Ready, Read!" *The Atlantic*, November 1998.

Mathews, Jay. "Success For Some," *Washington Post*, July 21, 2002.

Messing, Philip, Doug Wight and Carl Campanile. "Teacher Crushes Kid's Finger: Cops," *New York Post*, December 7, 2001.

Ravitch, Diane. *The Great School Wars: A History of the New York City Public Schools* (New York: Basic Books, 1974).

Stern, Sol. *Breaking Free: Public School Lessons and the Imperative of School Choice* (New York: Encounter Books, 2003).

Schemo, Diana Jean. "Rules Eased On Upgrading U.S. Schools," *New York Times*, March 16, 2004.

Steinberg, Jacques. "Schools Chief Calls for Loftier Standards," *New York Times*, January 25, 1996.

———. "Head of Board of Education Offers Plan to Require School Uniforms," *New York Times*, February 10, 1998.

———. "Crew's Plan to Hold Back Failing Students Has Familiar Ring," *New York Times*, April 26, 1998.

———. "Low on Teachers, New York Scours Austria," *New York Times*, July 11, 1998.

———. "Big Winner In Shake-Up," *New York Times*, June 25, 1999.

Walsh, Joan. "Clinton's Dumbest Education Idea," *Salon*, February 11, 1999.

Wyatt, Edward. "Schools Show Jump in Reports Of Sex Abuse," *New York Times*, May 23, 2001.

———. "Sexual Attacks In City Schools Are Up Sharply," *New York Times*, June 3, 2001.

Zernike, Kate. "Plaid's Out, Again, As Schools Give Up Requiring Uniforms," *New York Times*, September 13, 2002.

Author photo credit: Barbara P. Fernandez

Abby Goodnough has been a reporter for *The New York Times* since 1995. Now the paper's Miami bureau chief, she previously covered politics, the New York suburbs and, for four years, the New York City schools. In 2001, her front-page series "Ms. Moffett's First Year" won first prize in the series category of the Education Writers Association national awards. This is her first book.

PublicAffairs is a publishing house founded in 1997. It is a tribute to the standards, values, and flair of three persons who have served as mentors to countless reporters, writers, editors, and book people of all kinds, including me.

I.F. Stone, proprietor of *I. F. Stone's Weekly*, combined a commitment to the First Amendment with entrepreneurial zeal and reporting skill and became one of the great independent journalists in American history. At the age of eighty, Izzy published *The Trial of Socrates*, which was a national bestseller. He wrote the book after he taught himself ancient Greek.

Benjamin C. Bradlee was for nearly thirty years the charismatic editorial leader of *The Washington Post*. It was Ben who gave the *Post* the range and courage to pursue such historic issues as Watergate. He supported his reporters with a tenacity that made them fearless and it is no accident that so many became authors of influential, best-selling books.

Robert L. Bernstein, the chief executive of Random House for more than a quarter century, guided one of the nation's premier publishing houses. Bob was personally responsible for many books of political dissent and argument that challenged tyranny around the globe. He is also the founder and longtime chair of Human Rights Watch, one of the most respected human rights organizations in the world.

For fifty years, the banner of Public Affairs Press was carried by its owner Morris B. Schnapper, who published Gandhi, Nasser, Toynbee, Truman, and about 1,500 other authors. In 1983, Schnapper was described by *The Washington Post* as "a redoubtable gadfly." His legacy will endure in the books to come.

Peter Osnos, *Founder and Editor-at-Large*

CPSIA information can be obtained
at www.ICGtesting.com
Printed in the USA
JSHW022033250723
45290JS00001B/24